Jab Till It Hurts

How Following Gary Vaynerchuk's Advice Helped Me Build a 7 Figure Brand

By Ken 'Spanky' Moskowitz

Founder & CEO of Ad Zombies

This book would not have been possible without the incredible support of my wife Allison and my amazing starting lineup of Carter, Mason, Sydney, Josie, and Owen.

I hunt and gather for you. It's my responsibility, and one I don't take lightly.

Thank you, M-Team. You're my foundation.

Table of Contents

Foreword

My introduction to Ken Moskowitz came directly after I was told I should fire him.

I had been given the assignment to move to Phoenix, Arizona and help resurrect the media properties that our national broadcast company had recently purchased. They were a ratings and revenue disaster.

The building that was home to these radio stations looked exactly like the people felt and the products sounded—neglected, outdated, and battle worn.

After getting some initial direction and coaching from my boss and my peers on the leadership team, I scheduled weeks of brief meetings with employees, my new team.

In a dark second-floor production studio, I met Ken. I walked into his space skeptical of his value to the organization. Yet after a few minutes of discussion, I knew I had found one of my most important allies in the intimidating rebuilding project I had taken on.

Ken oozed energy, creativity, collaboration, approachability, openness to feedback, and loads of experience. Over the next three years, he attended virtually every meeting I called and was a critical member of a team that pulled off one of the most remarkable turnarounds in our company's history.

After celebrating the rebuild, Ken and I both left our employer at the same time, for different destinations. But we have kept in close contact as good friends over the years.

This book contains his remarkable story.

I now make my living as a consultant working with some of the world's largest companies. Three of my clients are on the Fortune 10 list. I don't share that information to brag; I share it for context since the chances are you and I have not met.

The companies I work with would love to have someone like Ken Moskowitz help lead them. He's that talented. And yet as the pages ahead describe, he decided to spend the last few years of his life building rather than running something.

What you're about to dig into is a playbook from someone who saw the incredible opportunity that today's Sharing and Membership Economies presented and decided to seize the moment. What he built—and is building—is no small thing, and he did it by giving and sharing. I'll let him tell the story.

Let me just say he's one of the most generous people I know. That means sharing his ideas. Sharing his wisdom. Sharing his creativity. And even sharing his house. Yes, being generous and *Jabbing Till It Hurts* to Ken and his wife, Allison, is so personal it has even led to them adopting children who desperately needed a second chance in this world.

When I told Ken about *Crush It* by Gary Vaynerchuk shortly after I read it, I had no idea he would listen to the book and then schedule a dinner with me—his boss—to let me know he needed to quit my team and leave corporate America.

I'm so glad he did.

~Russ Hill, Executive Consultant and Coach

Introduction

I never intended to become a pilot, but sometimes the unintended becomes the unexpected...*win*. I believe everything happens for a reason. More about this later in the book.

Let's go!

Have you ever flown an airplane? No, I'm not talking about standing in the cattle call line, waiting to get squished into the middle seat on a cross-country flight. I'm talking about getting in the left seat, the *pilot* seat, of an airplane, pushing that throttle all the way forward and rolling down the runway until you hit that perfect speed, the rotation speed, when you gently pull back on the yoke and *break Earth's gravity*.

That's what I'm talking about.

Sometimes you have to do things you never thought you could do in order to get to the next place in life. Sometimes you have to push yourself to a level of uncomfortable to achieve greatness. You have to step out of your comfort zone. But always, always do *you*.

If you ask any of my kids what I do for a living, they will tell you "My Dad writes ads," and they're right. I have been making a living pursuing my passion for over 30 years now. Thirty years of writing ads, jingles, storytelling. The only thing that's shifted is the medium of delivery. But I've never been one to be content with where I am. I've always wanted to go to the next level. To do something different. I'm always in motion. If you ask any of my friends what I do for a living, they'll have a completely different answer. They'll say I'm a dreamer. I'm a creator. I'm a visionary. But really what I am is a doer. A tester. A pusher—of limits.

I don't take the status quo as the norm. I try to create a new norm, every day.

If you're sitting in an office, working for some company you hate, completely disconnected from your job, just looking at the clock and thinking to yourself, "If only the day would end now," this book is for you.

I hope as you dig deeper into these pages, you find inspiration to push your own envelope. To try new things. To get in that pilot seat and take off, to wherever it is you want your destination to be.

I started following Gary Vaynerchuk around the time his book *Crush It!* came out in 2009. I thought it was a really well-done book and that it had a lot of value, so I began watching some of Gary's wine videos. I wasn't really even into wine, but I loved the value, the content he was delivering.

It caught my attention that he was delivering his content without asking anyone for anything. He didn't want you to buy wine, didn't want you to do business with him, nothing like that. In fact, if you watch his entire YouTube collection of wine content, you would think just the opposite—that he did NOT want you to buy wine from him. There are many videos, for example, in which he just talks about how crappy a wine tastes, or that something tastes like cat piss and tobacco. He was very, very direct and blunt with the consumer. But I think that's what endeared him to them and made them want to do business with him.

I watched Gary's actions very early on, saw what he was doing and thought, "This is really cool." He was growing a business not by asking for business but just by *providing value,* by jabbing, as he wrote in his third book, *Jab, Jab, Jab, Right Hook,* which is short or code for "give, give, give, ask." More specifically, Gary explains that jabs are "the lightweight pieces of content that benefit your customers by making them laugh, snicker, ponder, play a game, feel appreciated, or escape; right hooks are calls to action that benefit your businesses" (Vaynerchuk 2013).

In watching Gary deploy this no-nonsense strategy of giving, I watched him grow his dad's liquor business. Then, he started this new company with his brother called VaynerMedia and began giving even more value to people, this time about how to build your business and your brand.

Not only did I *watch* all the content, I also started figuring out ways to put it to use for my own business. The entire time Gary gives, he asks for nothing. Every once in a while, he'll throw you a right hook: "I've got a book coming out," or "Hey, I've got this event coming up, and if you want to attend it, here are the details." He'll only put out really, really small asks compared to the high value he brings with all of the giving, on a daily basis.

If you haven't caught on to this yet, Gary says the same thing in fifteen different ways, over and over again, every day. Yet I've noticed a lot of the world doesn't pick up on that. So, he just keeps repeating his mantra over and over again. Eventually, some people will get it. Sadly, many will listen but very few will deploy.

That really hit home for me as I started growing Ad Zombies, my flat-fee copywriting business founded in 2017.

Ad Zombies started growing because I was spending all this time in these Facebook Groups giving value, helping people with ad copy, providing them insight into the written word that moves people to action. All I would do was give, and jab, and give and jab. Every once in a while, in the Groups, somebody would ask a question about an ad, and someone else would say, "Oh, you need to talk to this guy Ken from Ad Zombies." My right hooks would be in the form of a comment like, "Yeah, those Ad Zombies are great." *That* was my right hook. The business started to grow and grow very quickly.

In just over a year, it's become a global brand helping thousands of clients.

I spend, *on a daily basis,* between four and five hours on Facebook and other platforms, jabbing— meaning, giving value. I'm helping people. I'm delivering content kind of the same way Gary does, in the space of copywriting and storytelling. This habit of giving has turned into a growing, healthy, seven-figure company, which has led to this other thing, me now speaking about how to grow a brand.

I'll never forget a time when I was speaking at the same conference as Gary in New Orleans—he was doing the keynote, I was leading some breakout sessions. I was feeling frustrated, so I asked him, "How do I get our clients to stop giving a shit about the *Buy Now, Click Here* approach? It never works!" Gary said, "You don't. You stand here and you preach. You're going to do it for the next ten years, and educate people, and some of them are going to get it, and some of them won't. But I love it! This is like a knowledge tree, from me to you, and from you to them. You're going to go on this journey now, of helping people, and teaching people."

So, that's what this book is. Me preaching the gospel of the jab, of giving until it hurts. I want you to see how giving and jabbing and giving and jabbing until you have your own six- or seven-figure a year business is the perfect thing to start doing when you're 45, or 55, or 65 or even 85. It's never too late.

I love doing this, spreading this message, yet I didn't even realize I loved doing it until I started doing it at scale. Jabbing is amazing. Giving value is amazing. But jabbing till it hurts is *remarkable.* You get so much more back than you give by jabbing and jabbing and jabbing until you've got nothing left.

When it hurts, that's when you really see the value of all the jabbing you've done.

When Ad Zombies started, there were no pre-set ideas about what this company would be, or what it would become, or how much money it would make. None of that. I'm not married to a number. But the successes came early and often for us. Those successes came in the form of customers and their feedback: *I love what you're doing, this is so great!*

I knew I was on to something.

Our clients give us all the information we need about how we're doing. Their reviews say so much. The wins aren't monetary, they're in the form of real responses to our work. Customer feedback is what lets me know we're doing something right on a daily basis.

The goal of Ad Zombies isn't to become the biggest copywriting company in the world, it's simply to be the best at what we do. Ad Zombies is the world's best flat fee copywriting service.

Copywriting can be very expensive. What Ad Zombies has done is figure out how to make it affordable for every business. We have an affordable solution for them because all of those expenses are spread out over all the customers, globally. The feedback we get from our customers? Those are our biggest wins. We celebrate when a customer puts a 5-star review up on our Facebook page. We celebrate it.

Today, as I work on this book and reflect on how jabbing changed my life and created my business, I'm standing on the beach in Mexico. This is my office for the week while on spring break with the kids. That's what I woke up to this morning—the beach.

Join me.

Chapter 1: 50 is the New 25

I don't think there's a right time or a wrong time to start a new business. There's just *the time*. Right now. Today. The opportunity to do something that you've always dreamed about doing is here. Often, people are afraid to step out and do what's in their heart, to do the thing they're passionate about, to pursue their hobby as a business, because they are either afraid of failure or, as in my case, they have a family to support.

Sure, stepping out on your own is scary. But that doesn't mean you shouldn't do it.

There's this false sense of security that a job is stable, that your salary, your payroll, is stable. *Yet jobs can go away at any moment.* We saw it happen when the economy contracted in 2008; it happens cyclically. Jobs are not secure. The only thing that's secure is you. *You* have the ability to control and maintain your own personal security and income.

I spent the better part of twenty-something years working as a corporate creative director. I worked for a big company, had a great job, great salary, great benefits. Nevertheless, I realized there had to be something more, I wanted something more. I felt like *I needed to do me*. I had achieved all of the milestones I could in my company. The only thing left for me was to ascend into my boss's role, and that was a role I had zero interest in. So, I took a leap of faith, and in December of 2010, I made the decision that it was time for me to go, it was time for me to pursue something else. I stepped out in my mid-40s to start Wedgie Media.

The thing that's scary for most people in their 40s and 50s is you have an established life at this point. You have a lifestyle, children to support, a dog, extended family obligations, a roof over your head. In my case, I have a wife and five children who require me to bring home a certain level of income to support our family.

It can be paralyzing to even think about taking that leap, but when you consider how much time you spend in your job, working, doing something for someone else, you quickly realize that you don't want to spend the next twenty, thirty years being miserable. That's what happened to me. I recognized that while I wasn't 100% miserable, I felt stuck. I was really good at what I did and no one ever saw me achieving anything outside that role.

They could never envision me leaving, let alone moving into a different position.

Feeling Resentment in Corporate America? You're Not Alone

I started to feel resentment. One of the big issues for me as creative director was the fact that I was helping our sales team close big, big, high-dollar, multi-year deals, and I never saw any return from that. The only thing I got was a good pat on the back, and an *Atta Boy!* while they were winning the sales contests and going on luxury cruises and going out with the clients. They were rewarded, yet I was the one doing the work, and it started to piss me off. Listen, you don't want to be in a position where you resent your job, your boss, the situation, whatever it is, because at that point, you're useless.

100% useless.

I remember being called into one of the sales meetings for an annual client, a large eye center. It was a renewal meeting. They were looking for some new creative, so the account manager said, "We need your creative on this, we need you to sell your vision." They needed me to do my song and dance. When I'm in a room with a client, I'm very much like Don Draper. I'm very matter of fact, and I paint with super broad brushstrokes so the vision is extremely clear and undeniably compelling.

I went into the sales meeting that day. The team from our company was there, and the team from their company was there. I looked at them and said, "This year, we are changing *everything* about the way you talk to potential candidates for eye surgery, because everything about what you do revolves around lifestyle. Clear vision, perfect vision leads to a lifestyle that people want."

I went on to unfold my campaign idea and how the year would work. I could see the room being sucked into the vision. I knew within five minutes that the deal was done. *I had them.* At the end of my presentation, the room went silent for about five seconds, and then erupted into applause. That was it. At that point, we moved to lunch and they had signed this client for a new annual deal. The money isn't important; the important thing is the deal was done and it was signed.

I felt great about the whole thing until about a month later, when an email came out to congratulate the top salespeople in the company. It mentioned some of the clients they had signed for renewals. The purpose of the message was to give the sales team great kudos and announce that these reps were going on this big luxury cruise to somewhere exotic and beautiful as a reward for their hard work. *Their* hard work?

At that moment, it really hit me. I felt so used. I felt like, *this is my work that landed you this annual freaking agreement and is making you a shit ton of money.* And all I get is a lunch? You guys are going out partying with all the clients and collecting that enormous paycheck, and it's my work that sealed the deal.

My friend and talk show host, Larry Gaydos, walked into my studio to congratulate me. He knew I was pissed and said "Spanky, screw them... you don't need them. They can't do this without *you.*"

It really fired me up. I was a company guy, I was willing to do what I had to do, and I was paid well for it. Yet despite the fact that I was paid well, I felt I deserved more because of the amount of effort, and creative, and ongoing execution of the campaigns delivering signed contracts year after year after year.

That bitterness really started to gnaw away at my soul. I started to feel more resentment every day I walked through the doors. Of course, that resentment had seasons. It lightened at times, it darkened at times. But one thing never changed—I was just the creative director, I was a cog in their machine.

I didn't enjoy being a cog. That really fueled me and drove me to make the leap from employee to employer—from working for The Man to being my own boss.

There are No Gatekeepers: The Internet is the Middleman

The Man is no longer in charge. Today, starting a business is easier than ever. There is no more middleman. The Man who used to control everything no longer exists. Today, the internet is the middleman and all you have to do is get on it, hang out your sign, and start your business.

Yes, it really is that easy.

It's simplicity at its best:

1. You decide you want to start a business.

2. You create a Facebook page for your business.

3. You create a website for your business, a one-page website if you need to, and your online business is now open.

4. All it takes are a couple of good first customer experiences and a few good customer reviews, and your business is on the map.

Your smartphone can put your business on the map tomorrow, so there's no excuse not to begin. The tools are right in front of you.

If you look at the history of my company, Ad Zombies, that's exactly how this unfolded. It started in a Facebook Group. I jabbed and helped someone write an ad. That led to people saying, "I wish I could write like that," which led to me saying, "Happy to help you, DM me, email me," which led to a flood of people asking for help, which started a business.

You can use Facebook groups to do business development on a daily basis. I still do. How do I do it? The key is this: I'm not going in there trying to sell them. I go in there as an expert, as an authority in the marketing field, which is what I am. I go into these Facebook marketing groups and I offer to help people fix their bad ads. I offer to help people write their copy and tweak things, because at the end of the day, the more value I bring, the more people talk about me, and the more they go, "Who is this guy?" and they start looking me up, and they discover that I own this business called Ad Zombies, which is a flat fee copywriting service. We write ads for hundreds and hundreds of agencies globally, we write ads for thousands of businesses around the world—small, medium, large, and Fortune 500. We write ads for some of the world's largest companies, and some of the smallest.

That's what I love about being alive right now. In a very short amount of time, using the tools on our smartphones, on our laptops, or on our tablets, a business can be born in a matter of minutes. You could have the idea this morning and have the business up and online before you go to bed.

That's how real this is.

Starting in Prime Time

If you're reading this book or listening to this book, and you're in that 45-55-year-old sweet spot that I call Prime Time, there's no better moment in your life to get started.

Let's say you're a nurse, and you're just kind of *done* working in the hospital, tired of the long shifts. You're over it, but you want to apply your knowledge, and use it for something of value. You could create the Nurse Hotline website to offer a Q&A for parents concerned about sick kids, or deliver valuable answers to questions people might have when they have this symptom or that symptom. Sure, there's WebMD, but perhaps *you* provide the more personal version of that.

As people discover you, and as you provide value in this space, you could have a big pharmaceutical company pay attention and go, "Huh, look at this super valuable site," and they offer you $60,000 a year to sponsor your website. Stuff like that happens.

Or, you could build your Matchbox car collection so big, so great, that Mattel—I think Mattel still owns Matchbox—comes to you and says, "We want to sponsor your Matchbox world tour. Here's $100,000 to go on stage and speak about Matchbox collectibles." That's really possible. The internet is the middleman today, remember? There's no more person in charge, no more gatekeeper.

It's just you, your smartphone, your wisdom, and your passion, that's it.

A Quick Word about MLMs

A lot of people are tempted to get into MLMs when they're feeling stuck or unhappy with their day jobs, but I'm not a fan. Multi-level marketing is such bullshit. Yes, there are consumer products that are great, but the MLM *model* is broken, it's messed up, it's wrong. You might look at it as the path to easy money, but what it is, in reality, is the path to easy money for the person at the top of the pyramid, *not you*. Stay the hell away from MLMs.

Don't get me wrong, I'm sure there are two or three MLMs that are really great and have terrific products and a legitimate payout structure. However, you are still not the owner. This is why I don't like them at all—you are not in control.

Do your own thing. Don't do someone else's version of that thing. You'll find your happiness growing because the money is yours, you're in control, and you don't have to worry about mandatory product purchases, bugging the crap out of your friends and family to join your "organization," or some "upline" impacting your bottom line.

Turn the Thing You Love into Your Hustle

As you're thinking about stepping out of your comfort zone and heading into running your own business, really consider what fires you up. What passion do you have? Whether it's working with model trains, or creating origami art, or flipping stuff on eBay, you can turn the thing you love into a business. But you have to have so much passion for what it is you do, it's effortless. It's like taking a breath. For me, writing ad copy is effortless— breathe in, breathe out, the ad is done. Where other people struggle with it, I don't. That matters.

As you're thinking about stepping out, do something that feeds your soul. Don't do something for the money, because *the money will come*. It will come! You just have to do what you love first and build your business around that.

I've always been a hustler, and definitely not in a bad way. I've always had a side hustle, something else going in my life aside from my 9 to 5 as a creative director. I had a full production studio in my first house. Thanks to that, I had a full second job that was almost matching my salary. I launched a DJ business at one point; then, a high-end wedding photography business. I've always had, in my DNA, something driving me to do more, to achieve more. It's never been a money thing, it's always been a satisfaction thing. It was about feeding my soul. At the end of the day, I needed that to be happy because I wasn't satisfied by my main job. My side hustle was what kept me alive during my corporate years so I could do my day job well.

As a kid, I always thought that I was going to be the number one radio disc jockey in America. I used to listen to the stations in New York City where I grew up, to some of the legends of broadcast radio, and emulate them. As a kid, I also found myself fascinated with commercials. Even though I would pretend to be a DJ and do time and weather checks, I found myself creating these commercials in my bedroom as well. When I was old enough and had the money to purchase some equipment, I basically created a broadcast studio in my bedroom.

While other kids were making mixtapes of their favorite songs, all of my mixtapes sucked because I would recreate *commercials*. I never dreamed that what I did as a kid would wind up being my lifelong career, and it's funny how that played out. Even though I now run a global copywriting service that writes ads, I never, as a kid, thought that what I do today was even possible.

The question is: what did *you* love to do as a kid? Maybe it's time to give that some thought.

Leverage Your Life Experience

50 is the new 25 because the reality is you've got another 40 or 50 years ahead of you. Our lifespans are getting longer. You've got 40 good years ahead of you, lots of time to do something—and if you're running something that you love, you can earn money and work at it until the day you die and never be dissatisfied.

To me, stepping out at 50 is incredible. Why? You have a vast amount of life experience at this point— such knowledge of the system of how things work. You have years and years of information at your disposal to work to your advantage. You don't have that when you first start out in your twenties; all you have is cocky arrogance. In your forties, you have a lot of information stored up there. A lot.

I think the other advantage of starting a business in mid-life is you know yourself really well. You know your weaknesses and your strengths. And if you don't, you should surround yourself with people who can help guide you. I do. It's the best thing about being the age I am. You have so much life experience and so much knowledge that you can use to your advantage. A twenty-year-old just can't keep up.

The Accidental Birth of Ad Zombies

Off I went in 2011, newly freed from my corporate role, and started Wedgie Media, a full-service creative agency and production company. It started out as a passionate pursuit, but over time, it grew to feel much like my job did, and I started resenting my own business.

I thought, "Wow, that's strange. Why am I resenting my own business?" Well, it was pretty obvious I was doing all of these things around my creative passion, but because I was running the productions, I became my old self again. I was doing work for other people and I stopped enjoying it. The fun part is creating, coming up with the script, the story idea, mapping out the shots. Creating is the best part for me. Execution? I hate. It's my downfall, it's my Kryptonite.

27

Still, I had a full roster of clients and I was building this great business. I was proud of the talented teams of film people we had assembled, and of the travel and filming television pilots and work on client websites and the big, elaborate marketing campaigns we were creating. The revenue was great, the projects were phenomenal, but I was feeling like an employee at my old company. In the back of my mind, I knew this venture was not exactly what I wanted it to be—but it was good enough. And because it was mine, it wasn't like I could walk away from it. My business was supporting my family.

Fast forward to March 6, 2017, when my newest business, Ad Zombies, took its first breath accidentally. As I said earlier, I was in a Facebook Group, Cat Howell's Facebook Ad Hacks Group, and the interesting part of being in Facebook Groups is that, depending on the group, there are different people with diverse needs and issues in their lives.

I hang around in marketing, branding, advertising groups; that's my jam. There was a guy in one of the groups I liked who was struggling with a Facebook ad. That Facebook ad was for a plastic surgeon, and it was for breast reconstruction, or augmentation. The ad he was using wasn't converting well. He was getting clicks and eyeballs, but little to no conversion. I jumped in and offered my expertise as a creative. I said, "Here's what's wrong with the ad," and I dissected it a little bit. I rewrote the ad in the comments section—that's all I did to start this whole new business.

This one simple act led to about 15 people saying, "Wow, I wish I could write like that!" So, of course, I said, "Hey, if you ever need help, hit me up. Shoot me an email, DM or whatever, I'm happy to help!" That weekend, I was flooded with DMs and emails from all over the world, because these Facebook Groups are global. They are everywhere, and I suddenly had this mass of humanity asking for copywriting help.

I thought, "This is great, people need my help. How the hell am I going to do this? I can't do this for free."

The funny thing, of course, is that I *would* do it for free if I could support my family off of free. I had all of these people who needed help, and wanted to figure out a way to serve them. By the end of that weekend, I told everyone who needed help that it was doable to write ten ads per month for the first ten people who signed up for a low flat rate. Wouldn't you know it, in about four hours every one of those 10 slots was gone!

At that moment, I knew I had something. I knew there was a business, an itch that needed to be scratched. I just didn't know how to build it in a way that would be scalable.

The Inspiration for a Memorable Brand

A couple of days passed. My creative collaboration partner Sean, who is now Head Copywriter at Ad Zombies, started texting with me that Sunday night; I remember *The Walking Dead* was on. He and I were texting about what to call this venture, this little thing that we still didn't even know what it was going to do, or what it was going to look like, or where it was going to go. But the company name evolved out of us watching *The Walking Dead*.

Originally, our slogan was Ad Zombies: Bringing Ads Back to Life. But it didn't really tell people what we do, and you'd have to think and burn some calories trying to figure it out. We quickly evolved it to Ad Zombies: The World's Best Flat Fee Ad Copywriting Service. The business was born.

Don't Settle for Less than 100%

Now, why do I love this business as opposed to my other company? The answer is very simple. With Ad Zombies, I get to do 100% of what I love. Let me say that again. With Ad Zombies, *I get to do what I love, all the time, every day.* That is remarkably freeing, and when you figure out what that is for you, your business can grow—and grow very quickly.

Earlier I mentioned my Kryptonite, so I think it's fair to also mention my superpower. My superpower is creative idea generation. I can go into a room of a hundred people, they can tell me about their business, and I can spit out branding, positioning, creative ideas within seconds. That's my superpower. Ad Zombies allows me to tap into that superpower multiple times a day, on a daily basis. Again, it's that passion.

When you have passion as the core driver of your business, it is unstoppable.

A Paycheck Isn't Nearly as Good as A Payday

This book is written for you. Oh, I don't know you, but *I am you.* I was the guy who was working at a really good job as a corporate creative director at a company that I loved. But I felt stuck, I felt like I couldn't go anywhere. Many of you are in situations like that. Why are you sitting at work? Why do you do a job you hate? Why are you working for an asshole? These are things you may be saying to yourself on a daily basis, but you don't articulate to others because you think, *well I'm 45 or 50 or 51,*

31

or, *oh, I've just got a few more years and then I'm out of this shit.*

But the reality is, now is the best time to start a business around whatever it is that fires you up, whatever it is that you're passionate about. If you're not living, and you're just earning a living, that's misery. Right?

A paycheck isn't nearly as good as a payday, and I mean a big payday—doing something you love that creates happiness and value for others. You can't measure the monetary value of personal happiness. When you get to do what you want, and live and work and eat and breathe what you're passionate about, you'll work your ass off, but it won't feel like you are. It'll feel like waking up on the beach every single day.

The thing that drives me is my passion for what I do. I *love* being a storyteller. There are times when I have ideas that I just have to write down, because even if I don't have the client that I can apply the creative to today, I will go out and seek the relationship so I can deploy that strategy tomorrow. Here's an example: one time a few years ago I was on a production shoot in Idaho with one of my all-time favorite clients, world-renowned architect Mark Candelaria, when my First Assistant Director Phil Click fell ill on set. We were going to take him back to rest up, but he said he was a little hungry, so we stopped and had pizza in Coeur d'Alene, Idaho. After we ate, I asked him how he was feeling and he perked up: "I feel better. I'm not shaky anymore." I looked at him and said, "Clearly, you had pizza deficiency syndrome." An ad concept was born. We sought out the pizza chain that then let us produce the Pizza Deficiency Syndrome ad campaign.

That's living your passion. Creative—that's what drives me, that's my thing. Your thing might be knitting. It might be decorative collars for hairless cats. Or beef jerky, a theme you'll see throughout this book. I like beef jerky, so it'll come up a lot!

Passion. Drive. Tenacity. These are all things that will help you launch a successful business. The other thing you'll need is patience and the ability to dream about what the future could be. Patience allows you to not be in a hurry. That doesn't mean you get to delay or hold onto those dreams for the future, it just means you've got to be patient because when things start to click, you'll be ready.

Dreaming big is important. I have a vision of where I want to be and what I want my business to look like—it looks like me running my company while I'm on the beach with my family. It looks like me traveling to Italy and having the lifestyle I want. To me, success is measured not by a dollar figure, but by my happy meter. Because when I'm happy, I'm successful. When I'm happy, business just runs itself and I don't feel like I'm working. Hustle ("work"), play, and family time all blends together because I'm living what I'm passionate about, and you can too.

Fifteen years ago, you couldn't even step up to the plate—you couldn't even get an at bat in the business world without getting through gatekeepers. Today, the gatekeepers are dead. You don't have to go through them. You can go around their lifeless bodies on the playing field. The internet has removed the middleman from getting in your way. Today, it's really easy to create a Facebook page about whatever it is you're passionate about, and connect with other people, and start building a brand.

That's it. Starting a business is that simple.

Key Points from Chapter 1

- Prime Time—midlife—is the perfect time to start a business because you truly know yourself and have more expertise to share than ever before.

- Don't settle for doing less than 100% of what you love, all the time.

- Jobs are not secure; the only thing that's secure is you. *You* have the ability to control and maintain your own personal financial security.

- Figure out what you have so much passion for that working on it is effortless.

- Remember, there is no gatekeeper or middleman stopping you from starting a business. With the internet, you can easily reach millions of customers directly.

Chapter 2: Don't Prepare, Just Do

People spend a lot of time preparing to do something, telling themselves "I'm getting ready." Preparing to write a book, preparing to start a new hobby. They spend a lot of time getting ready to get ready. All they do is find themselves preparing, and that's not going to cut it.

You have to jump in.

It's like having kids. People are never prepared, never ready, to become parents. They have all these questions: "Are we financially stable? Do we have enough money?" Spoiler alert: *No*. There are all of these concerns, and most of them revolve around money. You spend a lot of time preparing to have kids, yet you're never really *ready*. But when they come along, you just kind of figure it out. It's the same thing when you are starting a business.

People spend so much time making business plans and figuring out their corporate strategy or their mission statement. My God, the amount of energy people waste on their damn mission statement is ridiculous. How about you come up with your mission statement after you actually build something?

Take some action. Do it today.

It's just unbelievable how many people have the desire, or *say* they have the desire to do something, yet their actions don't map to their words. Open the door, step outside, and do it. Take the action first. It's not going to happen on its own. Water does not boil unless you put the burner on and crank it. Looking at it won't help. Getting ready won't help. Until you turn it on, it ain't gonna boil. Business is the same way.

When you first start something, you're taking a leap of faith. You're starting with nothing. You're starting from zero, which is where I started from with Ad Zombies. By the way, I took no money from Wedgie Media, my other company, to start Ad Zombies. It started on its own and it grew on its own, and it generated revenue from Day One on its own.

To take a company from zero to the trajectory of seven figures to hopefully eight figures is a remarkable feat. But it's not unachievable for you in your business. It *is* unachievable, however, if you don't take Step One, which is starting.

Zero Money Down

If you focus on the outcome rather than the income, the outcome will be the income. And it doesn't cost anything to do it. You could start your jabbing with zero dollars. That's right. Literally no money, just your time, and you can build a huge foundation, a huge network, for no money. It sounds like a bad commercial: "Zero money down!" But the truth is, zero money down can net you lots of zeroes on the back end. And by "lots of zeroes," I mean six figures. Seven figures.

It also costs nothing to be nice. Think about that. Don't do things with a motive. Don't do things with an ulterior motive of, "I'm going to drive sales." No, instead just do things to be nice. The more time you spend helping others and being nice, the more it's going to benefit you naturally. You don't have to work for that. It just comes to you. It's called karma, the way the world works. It's the ebb and flow. Give, give, give. And you will get, get, get.

Effective Jabbing for a New Business

Let's say you are a digital marketing specialist. You want to help companies grow their sales online. You've started this awesome little boutique agency, and you want to bring value to a community of roofers—roofers are your specialty niche, that's where you want to spend your time. There are literally dozens of Groups you could join that have to do with roofing on Facebook. *Roofers Helping Roofers, Roofers Asking Questions,* etc. Use the search bar, the search tool that no one ever uses on Facebook, and find them.

Just *join* those groups. Join them with the intent of helping them. Do *not* join them with the intent of selling them. Because if you do, you will freaking lose—not to mention, they'll probably kick you out. Go in and provide value:

"Hey! This is Mark from Wisconsin. Let me tell you that if you do XYZ in your ads, you'll get a better return on them because of X. By the way, we've done this for several clients and it works really, really well. If you have any questions, hit me up. Have an amazing day!"

You've not told them your business name, you haven't given them a phone number to call, you didn't mention your landing page, nothing. You're just offering value and information, and saying, "If you need help, hit me up." That's it. If you don't think that has value for your business, you're wrong. There is so much value in being able to give freely. Everyone should be able to jab till it hurts because it doesn't hurt to give.

Start with Nothing

Ad Zombies started with zero dollars in. It started with no website. It started with no Facebook page. It started with nothing. It was just me, in a Facebook Group, *helping*. I didn't ask anyone for anything. I was just giving them value.

You've got to be able to give, to show value, first. It's just a really a great way to start a business. Imagine if you were to take your passion, and go into a Facebook Group, and help other people problem solve because you have some knowledge other people don't possess. That's powerful. Super powerful.

From that Facebook Group I told you about in the last chapter, a little bit of revenue got generated immediately, within the first week, by me offering to write ads for people. There are website platforms today, Wix, Squarespace (I love Squarespace, by the way—it's the greatest platform ever) that you could, with no coding experience, no special web training, spend a half a day, maybe two days, putting together a basic website. Can you pretty it up over time? Absolutely. Does it have to be perfect right away? No way. It's better if it isn't, and you have some warts. Why? Because if you start documenting everything you're doing as you're building a business, and sharing it with the world, that endears you to people, to your customers. They want to experience the journey with you, the wins, the losses. It's all part of your story. Remember, a version one is better than a version none, too.

So, when you start, don't be ashamed to talk about the failures. Don't be afraid to talk about the real situation: "Hey, I'm not making any money at this," or of sharing the details of not understanding how the process of something works. If you surround yourself with enough good people, over time, you'll overcome these things and your business will start to thrive.

One is Better Than None

So, you've started your business. You've built a little brand around sewing, or gardening, or Matchbox cars, or antique designer buttons. We have an entire jar of buttons sitting at home on my buffet, collected by my wife's dad, and I see it every day, so that's why I'm thinking about buttons! Anyway, you've started your business, and you're in these Facebook Groups jabbing, giving advice, telling people where this button came from or that Matchbox car's year of manufacture, and the value of that car. You're teaching people about unique stitches that you can do with knitting, or how to have a green thumb even if they've never had a plant live more than a week in the past. You're giving value to these Groups in your niche, in your specialty, and now you have a way to monetize it, and you're trying to figure out, "How do I grow this thing?"

Eventually, you've got your first sale. You've got a dollar. But you're not very happy about it. You go, "Man, that sucked. I worked so hard, and now all I've got is a dollar."

I'm going to tell you right now—that dollar, that first dollar tastes so good that you want more and more. *Don't worry about more, that shouldn't be your focus. More will come in time.*

A buck is better than broke and zero dollars is what you had. So, as this business of yours starts to grow, and as you start to figure out how to monetize your brand, and sell your collectibles, or package your information in an e-course or an e-book for gardening or knitting or whatever your niche is, instead of getting greedy or getting pissed off that you've only made a hundred dollars in a week rather than a thousand, just know that with time, with patience, by continuing to add value to the world and the communities online that you participate in, that money will grow.

Remember, I started my company Ad Zombies in Facebook Groups by jabbing, by helping people rewrite ad copy, which led to the first transactions—

ten businesses, ten entrepreneurs just like you who gave me a hundred bucks a month to write ten ads for them. These transactions worked out to ten dollars an ad. That's nothing! But soon, it turned into a hundred people paying us $49 an ad.

Today, we have agencies all over the world that pay us a monthly retainer to write their ads for them. We have thousands of businesses that pay us anywhere from $49 to several hundred dollars per transaction to write their ads, their landing pages, their email sequences—all of the components they need to be successful in the marketing space.

Don't get greedy. Stay focused, stay hungry, and just know that the first dollar's going to taste really good.

One dollar is better than zero, and you're starting at zero.

Get Some Attention

From those first ten Ad Zombies customers, I had a foundation to work off of. That foundation gave us the money to build the website and to get a video piece done. Then, the big disruptive opportunity came: Infusionsoft was having their Icon Conference in Phoenix. This was a month after Ad Zombies took its first breath. I had previously arranged a meeting with the President and CEO of Design Pickle, and when I got there, I walked in their office, and said, "Guys, I want to know what you did at the Infusionsoft conference. What is it that you did that launched your business?" I wasn't sure of how they executed it, and I wanted to know.

The cool thing is, when you ask people, they're usually more than willing to tell you, they're willing to help you out. Successful people do not have the scarcity mentality. On the contrary, they want to share in your success, help you succeed. We should be doing that for one another constantly—giving, sharing, and growing together. They said, "Okay, here's what we did. We rented this pickle suit and this pushcart, and we basically just handed out pickles wrapped with our flyer. That's how Design Pickle was born."

I took a leap, and thought, "Hmm, what if we get some red bags, printed with our rudimentary logo on it, and our website, and stuffed the bags with a special coupon, a discount code?" Big red bags are like a walking billboard, and we needed some eyeballs on the company. So, we ordered the bags for the Infusionsoft conference. Then, my awesome First Assistant Director from my other company connected me with a zombie troupe—a group of people who are actors and go out as zombies. They're professionals, they're paid for this, but they're also zombie nerds, and they dig it. I said,

"Okay, how much is each of these people going to cost us?" I knew we needed more zombies rather than fewer. Right?

The morning of the conference, I had a horde of zombies with these bags, outside of the convention center. They were wandering up and down the street, handing out these bright red bags. We guerrilla marketed to get this thing going, to give Ad Zombies some momentum. We even had a run-in with the security of the convention center. They wanted us off the property, but I knew we were within our rights, because I had talked to someone at the Phoenix PD, and we weren't blocking anything or violating any laws. So, eventually the security team just let us do our thing.

We started. *We started.* That conference got us a lot of traction in the marketing world. We started picking up little jobs here or there from people who saw us at Icon.

We got people to post pictures and selfies with the zombies—the zombies would stop their act at the conference and pose with people. We took this bold leap, spent some money on bags and on those actors. We dropped some dough; I put it on my credit card. I'm like, "Alright, let's see where this goes." It wasn't like I was risking life or limb, however, or mortgaging the house to do this. It was just taking some money, and say, "Let's see if we can do something with this."

Between a small Facebook ad spend of $550, printing the bags and putting handouts in them, hiring the actors, and all the little extras, we spent just under $6,000 to have a dominant presence at ICON. The results were remarkable.

		Campaign Name		Website Purchases	Website Purchases Conversion Value
		ICON17 Retarget		252	$14,026.31
		ICON STZ Launch Push		1	$44.99
		ICON Save The Zombies LAUNCH		---	$0.00
		ICON 2017 Video Conversion		76	$3,771.25
		ICON 2017 Static PPE		10	$449.90
		ICON 2017 Static Traffic		---	$0.00
		ICON 2017 Traffic Video Views		1	$44.99
		ICON 2017 Video Views		18	$809.82
		Infusionsoft		---	$0.00
		Results from 9 campaigns		358 Total	$19,174.26 Total

Side note: I ran into Clate Mask and Scott Martineau at the Infusionsoft hosted cocktail hour and apologized for our guerrilla marketing tactics.

It's always better to ask for forgiveness than to ask

for permission. Be bold, put yourself out there, and be humble too.

Good Enough Is Good Enough

It worked. Sales started to come in. Sales started as a trickle, but they were showing a pattern. It wasn't big money at first, but it was something. It validated the concept for me. I knew this business needed to exist.

The first thing I had to do was start. Nothing was perfect at first—it couldn't have been *less* perfect. When someone placed an order online, the entire process was manual. It was a nightmare. Now, it wasn't a nightmare when it was five orders a day, but when orders start coming in the 50, 70, 100 a day range? When you hit those kinds of numbers, holy shit! It's devastating if you're manually processed. A sale would get transacted online. We'd get a receipt in the email, then we'd send them a link to fill out a creative brief. Then, they'd send the brief back and we had to match it up to make sure this brief went with that order. It was chaotic, but it was good enough. And sometimes, good enough is good enough.

Stop planning, start doing. You can adjust along the way.

Tactics to Try Immediately

So, there you are, sitting in your office, at a job you hate, with a boss who's a dick, and you're trying to figure out the answer to one question: *How do I turn my passion for Matchbox car collectibles into a business that actually makes me money?* I use that example, but it could be anything. It could be dolls. It could be artwork. It could be Rae Dunn ceramics. I know people who trade up Rae Dunn, who literally will go to the store, buy all the Rae Dunn stuff the day it comes out and then go online, on eBay, and flip it.

There's this one woman I know of who buys the stuff, and then, with her partner, sets up auctions on Facebook. You buy into the auction for $5. It's only $5, and you have a good shot of winning. They let it go to 200 people, then once it goes to that number, a winner gets picked in the auction to receive the pottery that cost them $30. They've collected five bucks *200 times* over! Do the math. That's a business.

So, what do *you* do? How do *you* get out of that job? The first thing you do, if you haven't done it yet, is set up a Facebook page. Now, I'm not talking about your personal page with pictures of your kids, I'm talking about setting up a business page. You can create a page for your business with any name you want: Matchbox Collectibles, Dollhouse

Collectibles. Don't agonize over the name, you can always change it later before you grow your following. I would also create an Instagram account and do the same exact thing. Give it a name and start posting pictures of your collection and talk about each of the items in it.

Start looking for Facebook pages who have like-minded individuals in them. If you go up to the top of the page, there's a search field. Search for "Rae Dunn pottery," or "Matchbox cars," for example. You start sharing in those Groups, *not selling*. For example, "Hey, this is my 1954 Matchbox blah, blah, blah." You give them a description, you share a picture, and you say something like, "Look at the details! What's your favorite car?" You'll start getting responses. When people want to connect with you, you can say "Hey, I don't want to take connections on my personal page, but let's chat on my business page." It's okay. You can keep them separate, you're not being a jerk by doing that.

Then, on Instagram, deploy a hashtag strategy. What's a hashtag strategy? With every post, the moment you post, the next thing you do is, in the first comment, you paste in the hashtags that are associated with the post you just made. In this case, you're going to search for hashtags and type in "Matchbox," "collectibles," and build a list of 30 relevant hashtags. That's your hashtag list for your new business. Hashtag every time you post on Instagram to get more eyes on your pics.

Then, follow people who are into Matchbox cars. When people post questions about the value of a car, there's your chance to jab. Someone might say, "Hey, I have this cool car, is it worth anything?" With your knowledge, you jump in and help by providing guidance. You say, "Hey, that car is worth $20, not $5." Or, if somebody thinks they have a car that's worth some real money, you might offer to buy it.

That's how you start to build your reputation, your credibility, and your—listen to this word—brand. That is how you begin. These are some basic steps that anyone can take for getting your business off the ground.

When it comes time to take orders, payment processing is easy. Too many people get bent out of shape about paying credit card processing fees to PayPal or Stripe, or Square, or whatever the app is that they use. Get over it. Every business has to make money somehow, and that's how they make money. It's cheap as shit and easy to set up.

If I sat down at a computer with you, I could have your business set up in less than 30 minutes. That's a Facebook page, an Instagram account, payment processing, hell, even a rudimentary, basic website.

Freaking 30 minutes and you're able to start taking money from people. That's how real it is.

Connecting the Dots to Your Potential Consumer

"There are not enough people out there to buy my product or service. There aren't enough people who would even be interested in it! And I certainly don't know how to connect with them."

This is something I hear, almost daily, from small-thinking individuals who don't understand the numbers today—the sheer volume of people who are online. So, how do you connect to your potential consumer? Let's say, for a moment, that you are a beef jerky enthusiast. You not only create your own jerky and marinades, but you like to sample and test beef jerky varieties from all around the world and review them as well. You also sell homemade jerky to friends, who are all saying, "You should make a business out of this!"

Let's talk about who will buy your beef jerky. There are, right now, 2.2 billion active users on Facebook. Think about how massive that number is. YouTube has 1.5 billion active monthly users. 1.5 billion. WhatsApp, which was just purchased by Facebook, 1.5 billion. Messenger, 1.3 billion. Instagram just surpassed 1 billion monthly active accounts. That's a shitload of people. Tell me there is not someone in there who will buy your beef jerky. Think about that. There's a lot of people you have access to through Facebook advertising who will buy your jerky. It's not that hard to find them. By the way, 2.2 billion Facebook users...that's way too many to hit with your soon-to-be digital budget, so let's say you just focus on the United States. You're still in the millions.

Let me walk you through how you build an audience on Facebook for your company and apply your specific niche or brand to the audience you're trying to target. First, go into the Ads Manager and create an audience. Let's call it Beef Jerky Lovers. Who do we want to target? People in the United States. Include everybody, but we know 18-year-olds probably aren't going to order stuff online, so let's target men and women over age 25. You can exclude people from the list who identify themselves as vegan—now we won't even offend vegans when we serve up our beef jerky ads!

Let's see if there's a group of people who like beef jerky. If you type in "beef jerky" into the targeting detail field, there are a couple of companies. You can target people who are fans of "jerky" or fans of specific meat or sausage companies. Oberto has almost a quarter of a million fans! People who like beef jerky? Over 5 million people. You create that audience. Then, you create ads and target these people: "If you think Oberto beef jerky is the best, wait until you try Bob's of Wisconsin! Click here to save 50% off your first order!"

Think about that. You've just created your first e-comm transaction. By the way, you don't even need an e-commerce website to get started. You can do everything through Stripe, PayPal, through Facebook Messenger. Or you can set up a very simple e-commerce website on SquareSpace or Wix—nothing fancy and nothing crazy expensive. Sure, you're going to have higher credit card transaction fees at first, but who gives a crap? If you're making $5,000 a week and you're paying transaction fees? Great! That's $5,000 a week more in sales than you had before you started. Be practical and look at the big picture, not today's picture.

Lots of people will buy your shit, and there are lots of people out there to buy it.

The Economics of Growing a New Business

Sometimes, jabs cost more than time. They can cost money, depending on the type of jab. For the most part, jabs are not going to cost you anything other than your time, your expertise, and that's it. But let's talk about the thing that everybody stresses about: "It's going to cost me a ton of money to grow my new business."

Not true.

Have you ever seen the moments, on *America's Got Talent,* when they have the three X's come on the screen? That statement about growing a new business costing a ton of money earns this kind of reaction in my mind because it's not accurate at all.

Let's talk about the budget of Ad Zombies when it began.

First, it started with a jab in a Facebook Group, which cost absolutely nothing. My second jab was to offer help to anyone who needed assistance writing ads. That cost nothing. The only thing it cost me was the time it cost to fix, to write, to help them with their ads. Time has value, but when you're starting a business, that's all you have to give.

It was only when I decided that I needed to make this service available to ten people that I decided to put any dollars into it. The dollars were used to build a basic website, a basic connection point where people could transact with me. That generated the revenue to build the initial foundation of the company. Not once did I take money from my personal savings or my other business.

I had a basic website set up that cost one hundred-something dollars. I did the entire layout internally, so there was no cost there, other than time. The reality is, I didn't even need a website. I could've done it all through Stripe, sending payment links without one person going to a website. But, because ten people had already said, "I'm going to pay you for this," I had $1,000 in working capital to play with. This gave me the ability to have more people sign up and purchase ad copy.

It was only when we started to have multiple orders coming in per day that we had the cash flow that allowed us to expand further and reinvest back in the business. Growing from zero to seven figures that quickly takes constant reinvestment in the business. It takes incredible discipline and 19-hour workdays. It's not easy. But when it's your passion, it is.

Key Points from Chapter 2

- Stop preparing to start your business. Just start.

- It doesn't take a lot of money to begin. Join Facebook Groups that cater to your market or passion and start sharing your knowledge and giving value to people.

- Build a simple Facebook page and website for your business; you can improve it later.

- Ask for help from those who know more than you.

- Don't try to hide what you don't know. Your customers want to go on a journey with you! Even your failures or mistakes are part of the story.

- There are millions and millions of people online at every moment—the opportunity is there. Stop thinking small!

Chapter 3: Scaling

If Google made a roadmap for how to grow a business, that roadmap would be called Gary Vaynerchuk. I followed a roadmap laid out by Gary, doing exactly what he preaches every single time you hear him deliver a keynote, or you hear him talk about deploying this on Facebook, or deploying that on Instagram, YouTube. He built the map. I just followed it and hit the start button.

After helping the individual with his ad copy in that one Facebook Group, I basically kept going into different Groups for marketers. Again, I wasn't selling my service or dropping the name Ad Zombies, which was still relatively new. I was going in there and just helping people. I would go to Tim Burd's Facebook Group, for example. Tim is a very high-level marketer with a lot of street cred, he's one of the best in the business. I would help people who were struggling with their copy. They would post their ad, and say, "I'm not getting great results, how do I fix this? Anybody have any suggestions?" Or they would post an ad that had been regurgitated a *thousand* times by marketing courses.

There are a lot of marketing courses out there that say they'll teach people how to start digital marketing agencies, but what they really teach is how to run Facebook ads and acquire leads. That means a lot of these small marketing agencies were and are struggling because if you only know the basics, you're missing the single most important element to successful advertising: understanding human behavior.

Are there good courses out there? YES! I know a few legit players in the space; in fact, I've been invited to speak at their private conferences and was thrilled to do so. Sadly, they are the exception. The rest of them are shit and simply regurgitate stuff from others.

I would go in and just start helping these people. Over time, individuals would friend request me and see that I owned Ad Zombies. It was everywhere; I immediately put it on all my pages, on LinkedIn, Instagram, Twitter. Anyone could see I had this thing.

I would, as Gary says, jab, jab, jab. I would offer guidance; I would be their Yoda.

I'm a big fan of Donald Miller's StoryBrand framework; I've built my website using this brilliant architecture and love what he says about stories. Every story has a hero, a guide, and a villain. I was their guide—the people I was helping would become the heroes. The villain varied. Those are the three components of any story, and I'd help them get the win. They conquered the day with great ad copy.

That is how I began to grow a following and a fan base. While this was happening, we had no systems in place. You have to understand that it started with me. I was running an entirely separate company, full time. Wedgie Media, my creative company, was serving clients, building web properties, filming television and video projects, and my time was really, really split. So, there wasn't a ton of time to think about *process*. I was just helping people write copy.

You Jumped. Now What?

So, you started your thing. Your side hustle is now a business. You're trying to build your income and replace your salary. But how do you get the marketing, the promotion done? How do you take the money that you are starting to earn and properly invest it in the digital tools like Facebook and Instagram, or Snapchat?

To do it is simple, but people overthink it. You want to approach it in three different ways:

1. **Brand:** You want your brand to always be in front of the people that most connect, or *should* connect with your product, service, or offering. You're not asking for sales, you're just present. You can do this by creating brand messages on Facebook that don't have a call to action, necessarily. They're not about selling. It's strictly engaging.

    For example, we run video ads in my company, Ad Zombies, at the top of the sales funnel. This is where we set a wide audience net and we *entertain* people. We have one where it's a clown sneaking up behind a kid, and it says something like, "You can't find the right words? We've got one for you: HELP." Then it says something about the world's best copywriting service. We have another one where it shows a young woman picking her nose, and it says "Picking the wrong words? It's snot funny. Pick us instead."

    We do this to entertain and engage potential customers, not to sell them. Then, when they engage with us, and those messages, we serve them ads that try to move them into the sales pipeline or funnel. These ads have a call to action: buy now, learn more. They have stories attached to them that help that consumer empathize or connect with what we're selling. It's not that difficult to achieve a robust sales pipeline on a platform like Facebook.

In fact, if you want to properly learn how to use the platform, you can sign up for Facebook's free course; it's called Blueprint. I believe the link is <u>facebook.com/blueprint</u>. You can follow the entire course from start to finish and get certified by Facebook. Not because you want to become a Facebook Marketer, but because you want to market what you do the right way. You don't need to pay anyone to do this, it's free.

2. **Engage by listening.** Listen to, or read, the conversations that are going on online about the topic or subject that you are an expert in. Pay attention to that conversation. My grandmother used to always say, "God gave us two ears and one mouth for a reason." We're supposed to listen more than we speak. So, listen to the online conversations and *then* respond to them thoughtfully. Don't just

jump in and respond; jump in when there is a reason to.

3. **Put marketing dollars behind it.** Once you know your audience, it's easy to go into Facebook, use some of the targeting tools that are available, and create a message targeted to those individuals. So, for example, if I wanted to get in front of people who follow Gary Vaynerchuk, I can find people, through targeting, who follow Gary, because he has a public profile. Facebook allows you to target people who follow public individuals. It's the same thing if it's Matchbox cars or beef jerky. You find people who like those things and suddenly you can get your message in front of them.

Start putting thought into your messages. Start writing messages in a way that gets the attention of the consumer that you're looking to attract. You don't have to spend a million dollars a year on marketing. You can start slow. You can spend a couple hundred bucks a month, ten dollars a day, twenty dollars a day. Start. Test and test and test.

Growing Pains at Ad Zombies

As orders would come in, we started having challenges. As I mentioned previously, in the beginning everything was done manually. This quickly made our inbox a total mess. Someone would place an order in our little online store. The email would come in for the confirmation of the order, the customer would pay either through PayPal or through Stripe, and a payment confirmation email would come in. Then, at some point, that customer would submit a creative brief, which was giving us all the information we needed to write the ad.

I say "we," but at that point, it was just me and my now Head Copywriter Sean Hughes, who has been part of both Wedgie Media and Ad Zombies since the beginning. So, when somebody would place the order, we had to match up the three emails we would receive to confirm that A) the customer had placed an order, B) they had paid for the order, and C) we had a creative brief for that order.

At first, we had rules set up in the mailbox that would paint colors on specific emails. Payments were green, briefs were yellow, orders were light red. It worked—until we started having, not 12 orders a week, but 12 orders per day, and then 12 orders per hour. Suddenly, everything was exponentially multiplied, so we'd be fishing through hundreds of emails trying to match shit up. It was a freaking disaster. A complete clusterfuck.

This went on for quite a few months. Having begun in March, by August, we were in a lot of pain. The orders kept rising and the internal disorganization kept getting worse. At that point, I decided to drop an email to Gary, to bring him up to speed on what had started by jabbing in the marketing community.

The Moment Gary Vaynerchuk Changed Everything

That email was the start of the change, *of everything*. I thanked him for all the guidance and value he brings to people like me, and wrote, "Next time I'm in New York, I'd like to take you to dinner, just to say thanks." Within five minutes (five minutes!), I got an email back that said, "Hey dude, I'd love to, but my schedule is *full*. However, I'm hosting this really cool dinner event and I'd love you to attend." He cc'd Kim Garcia on his team. Kim reached out to me, and in October, I wound up sitting at the table at the inaugural Digital Uncorked event at City Winery.

It was at that dinner that Gary gave me the advice that changed the trajectory of Ad Zombies.

This was the advice: He looked at me, as I was asking my whole list of questions about my challenges and struggles, and said, and I'm paraphrasing here, "Dude, you're not an operator, you're a creative. Just look at the way you dress. Look at your jacket." I was wearing a red and white striped shirt overlaid with an intricate line-drawn pattern, and a colorful jacket with a gingham flower in the buttonhole.

Anyway, Gary went on to say, "You're a creative, and that's cool, we need creatives. But *you* need an operator. What I would do is look in your social network, you're deeply connected on Facebook, LinkedIn, Instagram. Look in your network—I can *guarantee* there are at least five people in your network who have built a seven-, eight-, or nine-figure company. You show them what you've built *without* them and offer them twenty percent of your business for the potential of what it could become. The right operator is going to see the opportunity and shake hands on a deal." Again, this is paraphrased.

At that moment, I felt both relief and sadness. The sadness was in the form of this thought: "How could I not know this? How did I not realize that about myself? How was I not so aware that he was 100% right?"

The relief came from the realization of, *Oh my God, he's 100% right! I need to find this person.*

After the three-hour dinner, I went back to my hotel room, called my wife, our then-CFO, and I said, "We have to come up with a list of potential candidates. He says we've got this person in our network." We spent 90 minutes on a call that night. By the time we got off the call, it was close to 2:00 AM. I remember that distinctly. I was exhausted, and I was excited. We had a list of several names. By Sunday, we had it narrowed down to just a couple of names, and I started reaching out via email to set up meetings with these individuals.

That first lunch meeting was with my top pick, and our now Head of Operations, Brandon Disney. Yes, he's related to Walt.

Addressing the Challenges of Operational Scale

It was the end of October. I had just come back from meeting Gary, had my operations guy in place and was ready to start scaling. But we had no processes in place. I'd hired a developer, Red Cliff Labs, to help us build our relational database on a platform called Podio.

Podio is a platform I had never heard of until my friend and fellow entrepreneur David Tash introduced me to it. Podio helped David run his luxury limo company and his digital agency. There's a theme running through here: always surround yourself with good people and people who know more than you. That is one thing I consistently do. I don't play to my weaknesses at all. I give them zero attention; I can't fix the things I suck at. I can only surround myself with people who are strong in the areas I am weak. Any businessperson who wants to get ahead needs to do that. Surround yourself with people who are *great* at the things you suck at. Seriously, you'll never get better at the things you suck at!

Anyway, back to our story. Brandon, now only one day into his operational role, lead the call with Carson Young, the head developer at Red Cliff, and we started building the automation and process that allows streamlined, simplified flow.

I had an idea of what it would look like, but I couldn't really put the pieces together to explain to a developer: *here's how I need this to function.* I just said, "Here's the end result I need. If you could get to this result, that would be awesome." I didn't know how to explain the steps required, but Carson did a great job interviewing us, and Brandon is just incredibly operationally minded and very technical. He has a gift. If my gift is helping businesses tell their story, his gift is taking the most complex problem and breaking it down into the steps needed to get the results desired.

For example, I would say "I need it to do this, this, this, and this." Then, Brandon would reverse engineer my desired result after making me tell him, again, what I wanted. He would come up with a much simpler way to get there than I ever would have. Like I said, *surround yourself with people who know what they're doing.*

Brandon and Carson went into nerd mode on this call, then Carson and his team went to work. They created Version 1 of what we call the ADS system, the Advertising Delivery System—trademarked, fuck you, don't take it, I'll kill you all—the ADS system is built on the Podio backbone. What it does for us is magical. It simply allows those three emails that are required to process an order and puts them all together in a writer's queue. In the backend, it looks for those emails I explained earlier that we were matching up manually. In fact, they weren't even emails anymore, thanks to the new platform. They're like signals given from the different pages. I don't even know how it works, it's freaking magic, it's fairy dust and magic buttons.

I like buttons, and Brandon's made a lot of magic buttons for us. The process is simple, clean, and efficient as hell.

If you're starting something that has a lot of process needs behind it, you definitely need to have a good analytical person, you need a good system in place to handle that, and you need clean processes. If you're not a process person, find someone who is. Because without them, you're dead in the water.

Hiring and Training

Hiring is interesting for me, having never been, really, a boss. I've always treated people I work with more as coworkers. So, having someone in the operational space is valuable—having Brandon as my operations ninja has truly made all the difference for Ad Zombies. On his card, it says "Chief Make It Happen Guy and Magic Button Maker." He's a good balance for me. I live in the future, I'm a creative innovator, I think way out there. My thought process is so far removed from the typical person that having someone grounded like Brandon, who has so many years of operational and employee experience, is incredible.

Our Head Copywriter Sean handles most of the on-boarding for our writing team now. In the beginning, I did a lot of that and I sucked at it. I suck at many things so, again, I surround myself with people who don't.

What do we look for in writers or other team members? It's really simple. First of all, we want good people. I think you have to surround yourself with people who are good, who have a heart, who care. When I'm looking at bringing somebody new into our ecosystem, the paper resume means nothing to me. Everybody's resume looks really good; it's the best version of you on paper. The reality is, when you sit down to talk with a person, that's when you get a better sense of that individual as a human being and whether they're a good fit.

My wife will say I am IQ and she is EQ. Emotional intelligence is not my thing, but I read people pretty well, and I know Sean reads people pretty well. We look for people who are good first, and then after that, we look for great storytellers, great copywriters.

Our training is a little unique. Before we even train or let them into our world, we have them write some test ads for us. Why? Well, just because you're a great copywriter doesn't mean you'll be good at writing the way we need to write for Facebook ads, Instagram, Snapchat, Google AdWords. They require a different skill set. The reason I am not writing my own book, and I am having Laura Schaefer ghostwrite my book for me, is because Laura Schaefer knows how to write a book. I know how to write ad copy. If you switched our roles, we would most likely both fail pretty miserably at it.

We give them some test ads, and we see if they can fit into the ecosystem we work in. If they do, we have some training videos that talk about what we look for in our content writing, how we work through Facebook. We go through the things that they need to know to write well within the platforms we operate in.

Ninety percent of the writers that apply to work for us don't make the cut. We have three rounds of testing to become a writer on our team. Our process is rigorous because our clients are hiring pros; therefore, we only allow pros on our team.

Use Facebook Groups to Do Biz Dev

Since this chapter is all about scaling your new business, let's get into some specific business development tactics. Facebook Groups are, hands down, the single biggest source of business development for me and my business. Period. There is no place I would rather spread the word and get attention than in Facebook Groups. Again, I'm not talking about going into Groups and spamming them with bullshit offers to come to your business. No. Go into those Groups and provide *value*.

I can't tell you how many times I've gone up in front of a group of business owners or entrepreneurs or marketers and talked about using Facebook Groups for business development, and even though I say, "Don't spam," they hear, "Let me tell people about my business and give links to my shit," because some people are stupid.

First, you have to search out the Groups. Let's say you are a marketer. You work for a marketing firm, and you want to start your own. You go to the search bar at the top of Facebook, you go to the Groups, and you search for any kind of Group where you want to add value with marketing. Let's say you want to help homebuilders. You can go to construction contractors and find Groups that have 10,000 people in them—and those members are all people who own, or work in, that industry.

Start listening. Read the threads. Read what people are saying, what they're asking, the questions they have. When questions arise about marketing, jump in as the thought leader in that space. Jump in and add value. This is where you have to be careful not to pimp your business, not to get in there and say, "Hey, I'm John, and I run John's Global Marketing." NO. You jump and say, "Hey Jack, I see you're struggling with this. Here's what I would do," and give them some tactical, practical answers.

A lot of people are wired in a way that's like: "I don't wanna give them the answers. Someone has to pay for the answers." Screw them. They're not going to do it the right way. Because if that's their mindset, if all they're looking for is the sale, they're going to lose.

Spend time building a community, bringing value to others, and the business will come to you, and come to you, again and again and again. The minute you focus on the transaction, you're done. If you're chasing dollars all the time, you'll lose. It's not about chasing dollars.

Instead of focusing on the income, focus on the outcome. When you focus on the outcome, the income will come.

Offer value in helping people figure out their marketing. Offer value in teaching people about the collectibles that you know so much about. Offer value on landscaping tips, if that's your thing. You can *give away all of your advice*. Give it away. Because 90% or more of the people you give it to won't do shit with it. They just won't. I tell people all the time how to story tell and how to do things, and I give examples of how to write and yet they come to us and have us write their ads.

The other thing is, when you provide value in large groups, the payback comes at a scalable level.

People will do business with you because they trust you. Now, 30,000 people trust you, because you're providing value in that Group. Did a lightbulb just light up over your head? Did you get it? Because that's what Facebook Groups are for. That's how you build a community and build value, and grow your business using Facebook.

Between 2017 and the date this book was created, Facebook was directly accountable for over $500,000 in business development for my company. From Facebook Groups. *And this isn't by selling in Facebook groups.* It's just by giving value. I would give, give, give, ask. My asks never came—and still don't come—inside the Facebook Groups. You get kicked out of Facebook Groups if you spam your business. But if you're always providing value, you're going to drive attraction, and that attraction is going to lead to people looking at your profile and finding your business page. It all connects. It's the circle of life, Simba.

Suddenly, your business starts to grow. It explodes. It's exponential, and all you've done is do what you do and give advice and help people better their business. Half a million dollars, just from Facebook Groups. Did I mention the half a million dollars?

A Dollar a Day All the Way

If you plan on using the Facebook platform to grow your brand and you're putting videos out there, there's a great strategy I learned from Blitz Metrics' Dennis Yu. Dennis is one of the smartest guys I know in the industry and the strategy he uses to test is brilliant. It's called the Dollar a Day strategy. This strategy is very effective for testing what content resonates with your audience. To learn more about it, simply go to blitzmetrics.com.

What you do is you create your video. You record your truth, whatever it is—your marketing message, your why. Ask yourself, "Why do I do this?" Once you've created that video, you test it to an audience at a dollar a day. In fact, I usually test ten to twelve videos at a time. You see which one is driving engagement, is driving likes, is driving traffic. That isn't traffic to your website, necessarily, it's traffic to your Facebook page or engagement on that particular post. Why? Because what you can do inside of Facebook is create an audience, and then re-target or re-market to that audience that engaged with that video. They are good potential customers, and if you know that video is driving views and comments and shares and likes, that video has the potential to drive business to you as well.

Why a dollar a day? Because you could run ten videos at a dollar a day and, in a few days, discover your winners and your losers. Turn off the losers, don't worry about them. Keep spending money on the winners and amplify those winners. Then, run your targeted messages to the audiences that those winners have built. You can, in Facebook, build an audience of people who just watched that video. That's pretty ninja—a great way to build audiences for your business.

Grow Your Business with Instagram and YouTube

I've already talked about Facebook and Facebook Groups, so now I want to dig a little bit into other platforms, and how those platforms can positively impact your business. If you're in fashion or hairstyles, Instagram is a powerful way to get the visuals of your craft out to the world. What's really cool about Instagram is that it's a truly level playing field. If there's an influencer or a celebrity you want to connect with, and you have value to bring them (remember, don't just come at them with an ask or a right hook), you can DM—direct message— anyone on Instagram.

All you have to do is click on their profile. Then, in the upper righthand corner are three little dots. You click on those dots, and it shows a menu. "Send Message" is one of the options. Don't abuse the privilege of having that kind of access to the A-list of the world. Bring value. Show them you care. Offer them a free product or a free month of product, whatever it is you do. *Give.* Jab, give, jab. Don't ask. Give them something of value that makes them want to embrace what you do, embrace your business, embrace your brand, and get to know you. You want to romance the girl or the guy.

Instagram is a really powerful tool because it's a super visual medium, it's easy to advertise on, and it has millions and millions of followers, daily, uploading millions and millions of images and videos. Instagram Stories is a powerful micro-video blogging platform where you can publish short stories, videos that you can leave up for 24 hours. The ones that are really good, or have really powerful messages, you can save, and those are always part of your forever story. Instagram is a powerful tool for growth and business development.

YouTube

Not everyone feels comfortable being on camera. Hell, with my crooked nose and my not super-attractive face, *I'm* not comfortable on video. But I push myself to do it because I recognize that I'm a natural enroller. I can, with my energy, engage people in what I'm doing. There's a sense of belief and trust in me. Part of it is that I'm not trying to screw them over. My goal is to help people, and I think that naturally comes through when I'm on camera.

Now, how hard is it to build a brand around YouTube videos? Not very. Let's say, again, you are into beef jerky. You want to start your own beef jerky review business, where businesses send you jerky, you do reviews and then tell people about the best beef jerky from around the world, and that's it. You're not looking to gain anything from this monetarily, but it starts with you setting your iPhone or your Android on a little tripod and recording yourself. Talk about the jerky, the texture, the flavor, the spices, where it came from. Give it some information. Share with the world what it is. You might do, ala Gary Vaynerchuk, a three-jerky taste test and proclaim the winner of that taste test. Then you put the test on YouTube. It's not difficult to do.

If you want people to see the videos, you then promote them. You go into the AdWords platform, and you put some dollars into it, not a lot, and set them up as videos that people can view. You target your audience—people who have been searching for beef jerky, BBQ sauce, people who are into food, meat. You target people to see these videos and start to build a following. You'll find out businesses want to send you products because they're hopeful your review will help them build credibility and grow sales.

All you have to do is *start doing it*. Stop making excuses. Stop saying, "Ug, I'm going to suck at this," and stop *planning* to do it. As I said, a lot of people spend a lot of time planning but nobody spends time executing. They wonder why nothing changes. Get on YouTube. The only way to begin is to actually begin.

Pick the Perfect Platform for Your Performance

When you start your endeavor, there are literally hundreds of platforms you can choose for your messaging, and you don't have to use all of them. Sometimes it's better to go deep on one of them, and really dominate that platform for yourself and for your business, then it is to go wide on all of these platforms, trying everything. Not everybody has the time, not everybody has the desire, and not everybody is good at every type of platform delivery.

For example, I came from the audio world, and I really enjoy the audio platform. Audio is my first love; therefore, that's a spot that I'll spend more time in. For some of you, you look great on camera, and you're very outgoing and bubbly, so you might want to do video blogging. For others, you are writers, and you want to share your thoughts and ideas in the written word. Find the platform that speaks to you.

Don't be afraid to use Facebook for longform blog posts. Everyone is hung up on this idea that for blogging you've got to have your own website. Sure, great. But Facebook is a phenomenal platform for longform blogging. Why? Because everyone's in there, and long forms do get read. Don't listen to the naysayers who say, "Oh, people don't read that stuff, they just scroll on by." Bullshit. The people who are saying that are saying it because they don't have the attention to read stuff, but the reality is people who are interested in the topics and content you are putting out will read them. So, don't be afraid to use Facebook or Instagram for that.

If you want to create your own website, Squarespace is really easy to use. I think of all of the platforms out there, Squarespace is the most user-friendly.

If you are an audio person, use Medium, use SoundCloud, and create an RSS (Real Simple Syndication) feed to iTunes, and boom—you have your podcast.

When you pick a platform, you're not married to that platform forever. Don't romanticize your chosen platform, because when things change, you might get upset. Instead, test a few things. See what you're good at and see what works for you. Then, spend your time in that platform. Go deep and grow it. Sometimes people spread themselves too thin because they want to be everywhere, which makes them appear to be nowhere. When you find your platform, plant your flag, stake your claim, and dominate that space.

Putting Practical and Tactical Together for a Business

I had dinner with Emily and Sam Cataldo. They've had a family-run meat shop in Massapequa Long Island since 1967. In recent years, they added a Neapolitan-style pizza place to the shop called Saverio's Authentic Pizza Napoletana. I had met Emily through Gary Vaynerchuk, who had recommended they create a signature sound for their marketing, for anything they do on Facebook, Instagram, etc., so that when they run messages, the sound would end the message—an audio signature. Think about ESPN or PC Richards, which is a Long Island electronics chain. NBC, ABC. Signature sounds that are brand recognizable. I reached out to Emily and said, "I've been doing this my entire career, as a branding guy, and I would love to do this for you." I offered to do it for them at no charge because I knew exactly what they needed. That led to a further dialogue, in terms of, "What can we as a pizza place do, in terms of content, that makes sense?"

I recommended that they start with the low-hanging fruit: a branded weekly podcast. That podcast should be branded something like *Pie Cast*. So, we are talking about starting something branded Saverio's, immediately connecting it with pizza. What I would do with a podcast is record it as a video each week for YouTube and Facebook, then pull the audio out of it for audio podcasting. For the content, invite people into the shop on Pizza Monday's—invite all the local kids in the neighborhood, on the one day the shop is closed each week—and make pizzas with them. Show them how to make the dough, how to sauce it, and you create this local event that's free, where you're building goodwill. You build that high-level awareness in the community and you become a household name.

The other thing I would do on the podcast is share family recipes. They come from an old-world Italian family, so it would make sense for them to share some of their recipes and talk about how to make meatballs, lasagna. You create your own cooking show in the podcast. You create these little signature pieces that each and every week you're able to use as content.

I also recommended that because we were going to VoiceCon the next day, and they were trying to figure out how voice plays in to their pizza shop business, I recommended that they create an Alexa Skill that would allow customers in the area to easily order a pizza from Saverio's by simply speaking to their Alexa. "Alexa, I want to order a pizza!" The Alexa Skill would know that Saverio's is the pizza shop by default and say, "Great, what would you like on your pizza?" Suddenly, they started to see the value of having a voice Skill. Consumers could order their entire meal in three seconds and just walk in and pick it up twenty minutes later. That's how easy this could be.

These are just a couple simple, practical and tactical things that a pizza shop could do that would generate a lot of buzz for their growing business.

Key Points from Chapter 3

- As you grow your business, surround yourself with good people who have the skills you lack. You're a creative? Partner with an operations pro. You love operations? Partner with a creative.

- Giving value to people in Facebook Groups is a powerful way to do business development.

- Figure out which medium (video, audio, writing) you like the most when it comes to sharing value and telling your story.

- Spend a dollar a day promoting different pieces of content online and see what connects.

Chapter 4: Mentorship

I've already talked a lot about what a big difference Gary Vaynerchuk has made in my life and my business, but I wanted to devote a whole chapter to mentorship because it's just that important.

I first met Gary in New York City in 2014 at Lincoln Center. He was speaking at a one-day event with Dave Ramsey and Seth Godin. I'm not sure Gary remembers meeting me that day, but I totally remember the awkwardness of Dave Ramsey hosting Gary Vaynerchuk. Here's an uber-conservative Christian who, I don't think, has ever had a swear word pass his lips, with a guy who uses F-bombs like breath mints. I was impressed that Dave Ramsey, and his team, recognized that Gary was something special despite the style differences.

My understanding of Gary goes way back, and I have respected his honesty, his rawness, and the one-to-one relationship he has built with the people viewing his content since 2009. His YouTube presence was super small at that time; Twitter was his big thing back then. Instagram hadn't yet come to life, and Facebook was really young. I was following Gary way before he had millions of followers.

Anyway, I met Gary at that event in New York, and I also met Seth Godin there. Seth and I had a really interesting conversation on the steps of the stage at Lincoln Center. He said something to me that I'll never forget: "Spanky, what is it that you're *great* at?"

I looked at him and said, "Storytelling."

He said, "Then, do that. Stay in your lane and put the gas pedal down."

That was the advice he gave me. Now, I wasn't looking for sage advice, but that's where the conversation went. It wasn't until 2017 that I truly executed on his advice because of Gary's knowledge and content.

Lead with Gratitude

I am one of the thousands of people who show gratitude to Gary in so many ways for all the great value and advice he delivers, for free, to the world. I didn't go to Gary and say, "I have this startup, do you want to invest?" I didn't approach Gary to offer a stake of ownership, I basically just said, "Hey, thank you. I started this little thing by accident, it's growing, and it's because I follow the stuff you preach every day."

It was out of gratitude and thanks and humility that I reached out to him, and he responded. I think he naturally appreciates gratitude. When you don't come to him with an agenda, when you come to him with true gratitude, he responds well to that. That's why I'm able to write emails to Gary and get answers from him, and that's why I have Gary as a mentor.

The takeaway here is if there's someone you've been following and admiring for years, if there's someone giving you a lot of value, *don't reach out with an ask*. Just say thanks. You never know what might grow out of that kind of genuine gratitude. If you're feeling it anyway, why not express it to the person? We're all human.

Networking Like A Champ

Lots of people attend conferences, and there's a good reason. I don't attend conferences to go see the speaker and to sit in the breakout sessions at all. In fact, if you're going to conferences for that, you're going for the wrong reason. What you should be going to conferences for is to *connect,* and to rub shoulders with the people you need to connect with.

As you start down the path of building your business, there are going to be, inevitably, opportunities to attend conferences around your passion, your industry, your business. Find those conferences, and spend the money to attend them.

By attending these conferences, you will have access to everyone that's in attendance. Go to the cocktail hours. Attend the brunches. During the breaks, figure out where the traffic is. Spend time being visible. Make sure you connect with the people you want to connect with. Don't be the eye-darting leech that scans the room for your next victim. No, spend time with the people you want to talk to. Engage with them. Get their information, write their names down. Put them in your contacts on your phone. Start a dialogue with people, because at the end of the day every relationship you build is driving your network growth exponentially. Because that one point of connection could connect you to ten others—ten people who have high value for what you are doing. You just haven't met them yet.

Use conferences like a tool. Be social. Connect, connect, connect. If you're going to be a wallflower and hang out in the back, and watch people talk, you're going for the wrong reason. If you're going on the arm of someone, and think that just by being next to them you're suddenly going to be noticed, wrong take. Get out there. Say hi to people. Shake

hands, kiss babies like a politician. But mean it. Be
genuinely happy to meet people, and excited. These
are people who could potentially change the future
of your business. You just don't know it yet.

The Middle Seat Always Sucks...Or Does It?

I saw her coming down the aisle of the Southwest
flight from Chicago to New York. I realized very
quickly that her options were limited to sitting
between me and the dude on the aisle, or a couple
of rows back next to the bathroom. She wound up
taking the seat next to me, and I could tell by her
face that she didn't want to be in the middle
between two dudes and have to sit on this flight all
the way to New York City, but she sat there. It was
the best decision she made that day.

Sammy from Chicago is a stylist, a hair stylist. This
adorable, young, vivacious woman started chatting
with me when I looked at her and said, "Yeah, I
hate the middle seats, too." That broke the ice. She
and I started talking and I asked what she did. She
looked super trendy, she looked super fresh, she
had style—even though I have none, I can tell when
someone has style. She told me she was a hair
stylist and then started talking about her passion
and how she wanted to teach moms and dads of
biracial children how to take care of their

daughters' hair. She also wanted to teach dads in general how to take care of their daughters' hair—because most dads don't have a clue as to what to do with girls' hair. I'm raising my hand right now because I'm one of them, I'm that guy.

So, I asked her what her plan was to teach, and she really didn't have a plan, she just knew that she wanted to do something in that space. The rest of the flight, that's all we talked about. I started road-mapping a plan for her.

The plan we designed in the air that day included holding a free workshop on the Gold Coast of Chicago and advertising it to dads: "We're going to show you how to do your daughters' hair. It's a daddy and daughter workshop!" A one-day event, and it's free. She could use the salon space she works in or get a salon space somewhere else.

I told her that she could register hundreds of people for this free event, and what you can do is, if they all go away with a hair kit, charge for the kit. That way, everybody has all the supplies they need. It's really, really simple, but what it's doing is it's created an incredibly high-level awareness for her brand as a stylist and giving her a ton of street cred at the same time.

That was Part 1 of her plan. Part 2 is she wanted to connect with parents who've either adopted or, because of interracial marriage have a daughter who is biracial, and may not know how to do their daughter's hair. I said, "Why reinvent the wheel? Just do a separate event for these parents with a similar setup." So, you've got two events coming up, both free, and they both achieve the same purpose of building your brand.

Now, the thing Sammy has going for her that a lot of other people don't is that she's gorgeous, she's super outgoing, she's bubbly. She has a personality. You put that on a camera and people are going to watch. First, because she's attractive, second, because she's giving value to the world in terms of hair styling. She has a very, very specific mission and purpose.

Fast forward: On a recent follow-up call she shared some great news. Sammy found another stylist who is going to work with her as a partner because this event is going to go way bigger than she had ever thought. She is putting together the first event of its kind for this particular niche. This is not to drive sales. This is simply to drive awareness and to *add value* to the community. Period. That's how you build a brand.

Key Points from Chapter 4

- Express gratitude to the people who have helped and inspire you. Don't ask a potential mentor for help or investment. Just say thanks.

- Spend the money to attend conferences in your industry, and go with the express purpose of connecting with other people.

- Take a cue from Seth Godin and ask yourself, "What am I *great* at?"

- Be open to giving and receiving mentorship anywhere—even in the middle seat.

- Get specific about your mission and purpose, then figure out how to give value to people, whether it's online or in your local community.

Chapter 5: Setbacks

Don't expect miracles when you start your business. There are going to be early setbacks. In fact, there are going to be setbacks throughout your business life, and I'm not talking about setbacks of, like, a day without sales. I'm talking about weeks or months when shit just goes stagnant.

When that happens, people tend to go on the defense. What they do is, they tend to stop doing all the things that brought them early success. They go in the opposite direction and they start right hooking or trying to sell, because they're getting desperate, and desperation leads people to do stupid shit. Instead, embrace the setbacks and recognize that there are things you might have shifted or changed. Get back to the basics of doing what you did to launch your new business.

- Expect setbacks.

- Don't be thrown by them.

- Understand that it's part of the cycle, it's part of the ebb and flow of business.

You are not infallible, your business is not bulletproof, and there's a learning curve for all of us. Don't let those moments of setback get you down. When shit isn't working the way it used to, look at the way you've engineered your process. Say, "Hey, what's changed? Am I doing something different? Did the market change?"

Always, always stay on the offense. Jab, jab, jab. Give, give, give.

If you take any advice from this book, all you have to do is remember the title: jab 'till it hurts. *Because that is how you're going to win.* Bring so much value that you *suffocate* the negative, the conversation about whatever's going on. Keep jabbing.

Making Things Right

Mistakes happen; we all make mistakes. It's not like you're going to start your business and it's going to be perfect right out of the gate. But if you fuck it up, fix it up.

You're going to have an unhappy customer, a complaint on Facebook, a bad review left on Google, you just *will*—but how you respond will determine a ton about the future success of your business. If you ignore a bad review and let it fester that tells the world one thing: "I don't give a shit about my customers."

But if you respond in a thoughtful fashion, you can turn it around. Let's say the customer is not happy with the quality of the product, and you respond, "Hey Josh, I'm really sorry you're not happy with this. We're going to DM you, we want to find out what's wrong." Then, afterward, you can go back onto the post and say, "We were able to contact the customer and resolve the issue." Ask the customer to come back and explain that the issue was resolved, and they were happy.

Ignoring the bad review or negative feedback is an endorsement of that feedback. If you take a positive approach to managing your reputation as a business, you're going to win. You're going to win every single time.

Own your mistakes. Every business makes them. Turn your pissed off customers into raving fanatics and you can change the narrative of an unhappy customer with a bad experience. It's really that easy. So again, if you fuck it up, fix it up.

Trolls and Haters

Some of the setbacks you experience as you build your business are going to come in the form of trolls and haters. Let's face it, the internet has created a space where people feel safe saying shit they would never say to your damn face. They hide under the anonymity of the internet.

You have to be able to embrace the hate. When I say "embrace the hate," I mean that as trolls develop and find you, and they will, you have to learn the difference between trolls and haters versus legitimate negative reviews. What I've started doing is I thank them for their feedback, which really pisses them off. But I go no further than that, and I don't let them get under my skin anymore. What you need to do is embrace them, because there are trolls no matter what. Just be aware that getting trolled isn't bad, it just means you have a growing online presence. In fact, I'd be more concerned if you never got trolled.

Someone's going to tell you that your Matchbox collection sucks, that you know nothing about Rae Dunn, or that you don't know shit about beef jerky or artwork. Your response can be, "Thanks! Appreciate the feedback. Have a great day."

Suffocate the negative.

To a lot of people, trolls are perceived as a serious setback. No. Trolls mean you're winning. Trolls mean you're doing something right because you've got people's attention. Suffocate that negative and learn to ignore the noise. If you have setbacks along your journey, reach out to me. Chat with me. I'd love to talk to you. I can't help everybody, but I'll do my best to connect.

By the way, that's a jab.

Operational Hiccups

The earliest setbacks in Ad Zombies' growth were all related to me. I created my own roadblocks because I didn't understand the process world. What I did, and I wasted way more hours than I should have, was try to create a "process" that really wasn't a process. It was me monkeying with the system, or how emails flowed, or how we delivered ads. I spent a lot of time on customer experience.

I was trying to create the perfect customer experience, and the perfect customer experience to our customer is just delivering the freaking ad copy. That's it, it's really simple. Good ad copy, that's it. They don't care how it's wrapped, they don't care if it's pretty. They just want ad copy, because that's their pain point. Yet I spent a shitload of time trying to perfect the visuals, what people saw when they ordered from us. It was a disaster. As soon as I stopped doing that, and got out of my own way, things got a lot better and smoother. It didn't hurt that I had an operational ninja, in Brandon, who had previously built a multi-million-dollar business.

It's a Chess Game

There are games you play as a child that are very short—Clue, Chutes & Ladders—but none of them are like chess. Chess is a game of strategy and patience. Determining your every move, your every decision, hopefully allows you to eventually checkmate whomever it is you're playing against.

The strategy you deploy today for your business isn't for today's results; it's for tomorrow's checkmate. Every decision you make needs to take into account that *everything you do will be seen by everyone*. When you get on social media, you've got to avoid talking about politics. I don't care if you're Right or Left. If you post about it, you're going to divide half of your potential customers, and keep them away from you, keep them from doing business with you. It's a polarizing and unnecessary conversation to have. This is a business conversation. Politics does not mix into this.

When you are publishing stuff on Facebook and you're publishing your content on YouTube and Instagram, remember that it's going to be there for everyone to see and it's forever. Put some thought behind what you put out. Take some time to think before you act. If you're documenting, that's fine. Documenting is just following the process and the story as you go. But if you're putting out thoughtful content that needs to be decisive and have action, think about what you post before you post it. In this chess game, you will lose if you piss off people because you're dividing them due to personal feelings.

You have to make strategic moves and strategic decisions to move your business forward. But you can also make decisions that hurt it. And what I've talked about here in this section is one of them.

Plan B

Always have a Plan B. You never know when shit's gonna hit the fan. Things can go south. Plan for it. It'll happen, it always does.

It was just before the July 4th holiday weekend, and days before I was scheduled to leave for California for my family vacation, when I found out Brandon, my magic button maker, was in a serious car accident in Idaho. He and his son Blake were in Idaho for Blake's wakeboarding competition, when a missed stop sign caused a 55 mph collision and sent both of them to the hospital. Brandon ended up being transported to a Level 1 trauma center.

In the days that followed, I knew Brandon was hurt and out of commission. I knew that he had punctured a lung, fractured ribs, all sorts of things that take a toll on the human body. But I was thankful that he and his son were not killed in this accident. It was that bad.

Brandon wasn't ready to be bombarded with operational problems as he recovered from this accident, so I had to switch gears and put on my 360-degree creative, operations, and everything hat for several weeks to give Brandon the necessary time to heal. The goal was not to bother him with minutiae.

What I discovered at that moment was while we have backup systems for our automation, and we have redundancies in so many areas of our business, we didn't have a Plan B for the worst-case scenario. What if one of your key people is injured or, God forbid, killed? What is your back up plan? Does everyone know where everything is? Does everyone know how to access the files? Edit things? Get in the backend of systems?

You have to have a Plan B at all times.

That was something we didn't have for this scenario. Because how would you ever think that this scenario would come to pass? You don't. We don't think about our mortality. All we think about is the day-to-day functioning and operation of our lives. And then we're smacked in the face with a dose of mortality. So, I beg of you, I implore you, as you build your business, make sure that the trusted ones around you know the ins and outs of your business, so that should anything happen—should the unthinkable happen—business doesn't shut down because of one person.

Dealing with the Dark Days

In 2018, the word *entrepreneur* is so overused and so glamorized; everyone wants to be an entrepreneur. You'll see it in their Facebook profiles and their Instagram, "Look at me, I'm an entrepreneur!" with their 100-dollar bills and their photoshopped Lamborghinis.

Entrepreneurship is glamorized and idolized, but there are things about being an entrepreneur that people don't talk about. I talk about it because it's a real thing for me and it's heavy—and that is the isolation and the loneliness of entrepreneurship. There aren't many people wired the way you are wired or the way I am wired. Entrepreneurs have certain traits, and so you can go deep and go by yourself, and do things, and take the reins, and create something because that's *who you are,* that's part of your soul. But the side of entrepreneurship that people don't talk about is the *loneliness*. When you are building your own business, man, there are a lot of people who want to give you advice, but no one is there when you are working on this thing by yourself, when you're up against a brick wall in the middle of the night, and you're experiencing nothing but hardship, heartache, and heartburn... and none of the joy.

Entrepreneurship is glamorized like it's the best thing ever and you're going to make a billion dollars, and they forget to talk about the people who are sitting there depressed in their office contemplating suicide. Ninety-nine percent of the time I love life, I just do, but I'd be lying to you if I didn't tell you that the thought has crossed my mind—that the darkness has crept in, and I've thought, *I just can't do this anymore.* It's lonely and isolating, and I think the worst part of it is, there really aren't that many people wired like this. The ones who say they are, really aren't, because when you reach out to people who claim to be entrepreneurs, they don't know what you're talking about. Instead, they're all hype: "I've got my job, and I've got my side hustle, and I've got my e-com, my Alibaba drop ship deal going, and I'm making money, I'm rolling in it!" But they really aren't; it's just the story they're telling everyone. They don't talk about the darkness, the isolation.

Sitting in an office sometimes, by yourself, with your own thoughts, is the scariest freaking thing ever. Because your mind can *really fuck with you.* A lot of people don't talk about this because it's dark and ugly, but it needs to be talked about because entrepreneurs have one of the highest suicide rates of any segment of the population.

You know, when you sit somewhere by yourself eight, 10, 12, 18 hours a day, you've got nothing but you and your thoughts. With entrepreneurship, you can have really high highs, and within minutes or hours, you can have crashing lows, just based on the cycle of where the business is.

I had a business consultant who, as we were growing my other company said, "Hey, you've got to stop doing *that* and start focusing on *this,* because every time you go *here,* the business gets smaller. When you become a doer instead of an entrepreneur, the business contracts. You have to grow, so you do, but then you stop and become a worker bee and the business contracts."

When you go through those cycles, it beats the shit out of you emotionally. You think you're never going to get this right and you're never going to amount to whatever it is you think you should amount to with this business. *It's as isolating as hell* because you can't talk to people about this.

Nobody understands. Your friends who are working some 9 to 5 job with some company have *no idea*. They're done with their workday, and they're going to their daughter's dance recital. They're not building something for the future, they're building something for somebody else's future. It's really hard to have a conversation with them because they can't relate. I have many friends who can't relate to the fact that I would start my day at 5 AM and go to bed at 11 or push to midnight; they can't comprehend that.

They can't comprehend not being able to sit down with your spouse and binge watch, on a weekend, whatever it is they want to watch. I will not sit and watch baseball games because they're too long. I'm not going to dedicate my life to watching sports on TV or binge watching a show when I've got an empire to build. So, as you're growing your business you do isolate yourself, you become very insular—not because you don't want to be social, but because you're building something and you're jazzed about it.

You might have an extraordinary sales day, whatever extraordinary is to you, and then you get one pissed off customer email and that totally brings you down. Running your own business? I envision it as what bipolar people go through—incredible highs followed by crashing lows. Entrepreneurship is like that. Between those highs are these deep, dark valleys—valleys you can get lost in very easily.

Reach Out and Connect

I encourage you, if you're reading this book or listening to this book, and you're an entrepreneur and you're feeling that darkness right this moment, connect with me. Reach out to me, DM, Facebook, whatever. It doesn't matter. Connect with me. Don't go it alone, because you could get yourself into a dark hole that you can't get out of, and you deserve better than that. You just do.

When you're sinking, what you need to do is extract yourself from that situation in that moment. Get out of the cave in your house, or the office you occupy. Get out of there. Call a friend, get together with humans. This is such an isolating and lonely game, no matter who you are. Look, even some of the most successful entrepreneurs in the world experience loneliness and darkness. Why? Because no one thinks like us, except us. Other entrepreneurs can relate to the feelings, to where you are, today, in this moment. The average person who has a job, who doesn't aspire to do something outside of the box? That person can't relate to what you're doing, to where you are with your business. They just can't, they don't live in this world. When things get dark, and it's lonely, don't wallow. Don't sit there in that darkness. Stop what you're doing and get out and interact with the world.

If one of my kids was starting a business and sitting in the cave I'm talking about here, the advice I would give them is to simply make sure, as you go through these waves, these dark periods as you're starting your business, that you have your core, a solid foundation of friends who understand you, who know you. They may not be in the same place as you, but these are people who will drop everything to go grab a beer with you. When you have those dark moments, you need to shake them off quickly by extracting yourself from the situation.

As your business grows and you taste success, the dark days don't lessen, but I can say that the highs become higher and the lows stay the same. So, it feels like you're much happier, but you still have those dark moments. Just the other day, we had a customer in an online chat who was being incredibly difficult. The saying is, "The customer is always right," but I'm going to tell you, that's bullshit. The customer is not always right—they think they're always right, but there are times the customer is wrong. You have to educate them. As a business owner, your job is to clarify a situation for them so they understand their options. This customer was being such a difficult person and I felt so beat down by the end of this conversation.

This came at the end of a day in which we had *extraordinary* sales. Like, sales that make you jump and high five. Those highs...just get higher. The lows don't get any lower.

Ten years ago, my struggle was different. When I was an employee it was, "How quickly can I get the hell out of the office, so I can get home?" My depression came in the form of salespeople turning stuff in on a Friday right before a holiday weekend. While they were sipping margaritas poolside, I was stuck at the office doing creative. That's the difference.

Today, it's all self-generated. It's not somebody else imposing their will on my life. It's me and *my business*. The darkness is different. It used to be resentment. Now it's just cyclical waves of business.

Entrepreneurship and Relationships

I have been married to this incredibly patient woman, Allison, since 1995. And I will tell you, I don't know how she puts up with me, because I can have an incredibly amazing day, and then the next moment something goes south, and I can go in completely the opposite direction. I am on this rollercoaster of happy-sad, happy-sad, happy-sad. Joyous, grumpy. You go from standing on top of the mountain with your hands on your hips like a superhero to the next moment, where you're in the fetal position on the ground feeling like, "This'll never work."

Having a spouse who understands who you are is so vital. If you're in a relationship with someone who is trying to change you or mold you to who they think you should be, it's not a good relationship for anyone, but for an entrepreneur, it's a death sentence. You have to be you, you have to be flexible, you have to be free-thinking.

My wife gives me the air cover, on a daily basis, to do *what I do* in my business. But at the same time, she pays the consequences for it. Eighteen-hour days take their toll, especially when you have a family with five kids. My work days sometimes kill our family time. That's not to say I don't go to my children's soccer games, or football games, or orchestra performances. But my work is my life, my passion. My work is my rocket fuel. I can't breathe without it.

Building a business like this is hard work. Having a partner, a spouse, who understands the journey, who understands the work that goes into it to be able to reap the rewards down the road is critical. If you don't have that person in your life, if you're trying to do this with someone who doesn't understand, that relationship is going to crumble, it's just going to fall apart.

Successful Businesses and Entrepreneurial Failures

Whether a business is a success or a failure is determined by the individual. A company doesn't have to make $10 million or $100 million a year to be successful if your goal is to provide an income for your family that is equal to or slightly above what you were making in the corporate world. You may only need $70,000 a year to support your family, so a business that generates this amount is successful.

I believe there are more successful businesses all around us than most people realize, but I also think that a lot of people have unrealistic goals and expectations of what their business could be or should generate in terms of revenue. If Ad Zombies never grew above a $500,000 a year company, that would be fine. Because what that would do is support my family and my internal team enough that everybody could make a living and be happy doing what they do.

Success doesn't always equal millions and millions of dollars. Now, if your business gets there, great! Congratulations! But don't go in expecting to just crush the shit out of it and make $10 million. I had zero, ZERO expectations that Ad Zombies would become anything because it was an accident. The fact that it was able to provide a stable income, and then several stable incomes for team members, is remarkable. Is the business successful? Absolutely. Would I be upset if the business never grew beyond what it is today? Not at all.

Success is in the mind of the individual. Success is not some magic number that we strive for. No matter how much business my company does, or how much growth, I pay myself a very modest salary to comfortably support my family. The rest gets reinvested back in the business. You don't have to get crazy to blow all your money or start living like a king.

Will my salary change? Sure, absolutely. I think you find the financial point you need to be happy. That set point, whether it's money or work-life balance or whatever.

Wantrepreneurs and Opportuneurs

Today, the word *entrepreneur* is used very loosely. Too often, people call themselves entrepreneurs when they're really wantrepreneurs. I still don't call myself an entrepreneur. A lot of people look at me that way, but I consider myself a guy who started a business and is grinding and hustling and doing what he's gotta do to grow it. I have a lot of entrepreneurial tendencies, and I think it's either in your DNA or it's not. I don't think you can teach people how to be entrepreneurs.

Some people are opportuneurs, not entrepreneurs. An entrepreneur sees something and realizes there's a market and creates something to fill a need. An opportuneur just looks for every opportunity to cash in and make money. They go in with the mindset of, "I'm going to crush it and make a bazillion dollars!" As soon as they taste a little success, they get flashy. They go buy a car they can't afford, watches they don't need, they get really fancy with their homes, and start to burn through that money. Just like an athlete newly signed to an NFL contract.

When things start to go south, there's no reserve, there's nothing left in the tank because all they've done is burn through every penny they've made. They're really not setting themselves for a long-term profitable, financially sound business. They're setting themselves up for quick hits, like a junkie. They get a hit of heroin, and it feels good, but then they need more heroin. If you build this thing right and build this thing slowly, it'll feed you for decades. In many businesses, it'll feed generations.

Nothing Fixes Broken

This is going to be a hard pill for many to swallow, but nothing fixes a broken mindset. Nothing is going to fix your happiness, and often when people are chasing an entrepreneurial dream, they're chasing the wrong happiness. They're chasing money.

I can tell you firsthand: money doesn't buy happiness. In fact, recent news stories about Kate Spade and Anthony Bourdain committing suicide are further proof that no matter how much money you have, you *can't buy happiness*. Anthony, a chef, author, and guy who had his own TV show traveling the world, was one of my favorite storytellers, ever, who took his own life in a hotel room in Paris. You hear about these tragedies again and again and again, but it seems like only the celebrities are the ones that grab the headlines and get people's attention. If that's what it takes, that's fine.

Money cannot buy you happiness.

There are a lot of wantrepreneurs out there who are not chasing the right thing. They're chasing what they *perceive* to be happiness, namely money. In reality, money is only one component of the big picture. You can chase as many dollars as you want, but there comes a time when no amount of money in the world fixes your broken shit. I was broken for many years. I was chasing hundreds of thousands of dollars because that was my goal. I wanted to grow as much money as I could, or get as much money as I could, because I thought that that would make me happy. After all, if I had money, then I could go on vacations, and if I had money, then I could buy this shit, and that shit. I could buy this car and that car.

There's this perceived value that is put on money when in reality, happiness comes from within. It comes from doing something that feeds your soul. It comes from doing the right thing. There's no external force that's in control of your happiness. It's all within you. I feel like Yoda saying, "The power of The Force is within you." Yoda was right. It really is. Instead of trying to build a business around a dollar amount, build your business around your passion, and the dollars will come. This is starting to sound like a theme, right?

As of the day I wrote this chapter, we just came off a horrific month in my business. We shed—that means lost—over $160,000 in revenue. *Gone.* If money bought happiness, I'd be devastated. But I'm not. It happens. This is what happens in business. You have cycles. We onboarded a lot of unqualified clients, and then two, three months into the relationship, they realized that they are in way over their head, and while working with us is great, they don't have the business to sustain the relationship with us, so they opt out. And that's gonna happen. It's called churn, attrition, and in business, you're going to have churn.

Shedding $160,000 to most people would be devastating. Financially, it impacts the business. Yes. But is it devastating to me? No! Because that's not what makes me happy, and that's not what should make *you* happy. What makes me happy is going to Mexico with my family. The money simply gives us the freedom to do that. But not the happiness. The happiness comes from being with my family, from going to amusement parks with my kids.

Money is an admission fee. That's all it is. It's not happiness.

Key Points from Chapter 5

- There will be setbacks as you grow your business. Don't freak out. Setbacks are natural. When they occur, focus on jabbing and doing the things that worked in the beginning.

- Suffocate the trolls by thanking them and then ignoring them.

- Remember, money cannot buy happiness.

- If you're stuck in a dark, lonely place as an entrepreneur, reach out to a friend, or reach out to me. I understand how you are feeling and I want to help.

- Entrepreneurship is not all glamorous.

- As you grow your business and experience more successes, the highs will become higher and the lows will stay the same.

Chapter 6: All About that Jab

It would be impossible for me to say too much about jabbing. So, let's do a whole chapter on it, shall we?

I've never felt like I give too much information for too little return when I'm jabbing because I don't look for a return from everything I do. The return, to me, is often as simple as a person having a lightbulb moment and figuring something out— because I gave them an insight they didn't have before.

Knowledge is not a commodity; it's not like soybeans or coffee beans. It's freely available to everybody on the internet; you can Google search anything these days. Schools are backward because they teach rote memorization and we don't need that anymore. We need access to data and access to people who will help us understand the data in a meaningful way.

I like jabbing. If I could dedicate eight hours a day to giving value in Facebook groups, I would totally do it. I enjoy it; I love making a difference in people's businesses. It's a high for me. I felt like I was on Facebook 24/7 when we first start Ad Zombies because the company was me—I *was* Ad Zombies. Fortunately, by Day 15, I had help. On Day 30 I had *more* help. Then I got real help when Brandon Disney, our Operations Ninja, came on board.

In short, I found that the more people I had around me, the easier it was for me to jab, which is what I want to be doing the most.

Give your help, your knowledge away. Help as people have questions about what you care about, about what you know. Provide value. Give, give, give. Once you've done that, it's a hell of a lot easier to say, "Hey, by the way, I have a new advanced XYZ course you can check out," or "Want to try my beef jerky?" than if you're throwing an ask out there without any history.

Start your business. Begin giving. That's it.

A Memorable Jab

One of my most memorable jabs comes in the form of an ad I wrote for a swim school. The jab was done specifically for a colleague and friend of mine, David Tash of Tash Advertising, who needed to pump up enrollment for his swim school client.

Why this is such a memorable jab is not necessarily how David implemented the ad with his clients, it's how *another* swim school caught the concept. That swim school reached out to us, and we created a different, albeit similar, ad strategy for their swim school.

Their swim school was having horrible enrollment problems and, like my friend David's client, they were using images of happy babies in swimming pools and trying to sell the joyful experience of swim lessons. The reason this doesn't work is because it doesn't stand out. It doesn't connect emotionally and viscerally with the audience; it's just wallpaper when you scroll through your newsfeed.

The ad we created was vastly different.

The ad we created shows a father and daughter standing graveside at a cemetery, looking down. The headline of the ad read, "Don't let this happen to your child." Then, over the course of the body of the ad, it painted a picture of what it's like to drown from the child's perspective. As they fall into the pool, they don't make a sound, no one hears them, yet they can see everything going on around the deck as the water fills their lungs. It burns, it's excruciating. As they continue to sink, things get farther and farther away. The child sees the dog barking at the deck, but no one sees or hears this event because a child drowning in a pool is silent. They don't make noises like you think; they don't splash. Slowly, the child sinks to the bottom, the light begins to fade, and he's gone.

As you can imagine, *that* ad had an emotional impact on the audience.

The swim school having trouble booking ended up selling six months' worth of swim classes in three days. That's how you get an audience to react. This ad is probably, to this day, my most memorable jab. This jab turned into something very powerful and effective—not for the original person intended, but for another company.

Jabs Change Everything

Jabbing has changed the course of my company. Ad Zombies would not be where it is today if not for my jabbing in Facebook Groups. However, as the company has grown, it's been harder and harder for me to devote the time needed to jabbing. This is a mistake. In fact, it goes against everything I'm telling you to do in this book. Wait, did I just admit I'm not drinking my own Kool-Aid? Remember when I said *admit when you're wrong?* Getting busy shouldn't get in the way of bringing value. You've *got* to continue jabbing even as your

121

business grows and finds success because that is what brings value to the community.

Continuous jabbing keeps the snowball of growth in gear.

When you are jabbing every day, and then suddenly you are jabbing every *other* day, you're still present. But when you're jabbing every four days or every month, it changes the momentum—the energy of the growth of your business, of your brand. You've got to stay in the Facebook Groups if you've established a presence and a good reputation there. Spending significantly less time in Groups earlier this year was the one oversight in my time management that I can't reverse, I can only course correct.

Don't beat yourself up if you make mistakes or if you need to course correct. It's okay, it happens to all of us. But jabbing and staying engaged with that core audience of people that have built your company, your customers, is critical.

As of the writing of this book, yes, my jabs have decreased dramatically. I've allowed other things to get in the way. However, that is not going to continue. I've started increasing the amount of time spent jabbing in Groups and I'm going to continue to do so until I'm in multiple Groups every day, jabbing and jabbing and jabbing. It just takes a little extra effort, an extra hour a day to do it. If you are consistent, your business will continue to see new explosive growth long-term.

Leveraging the Power of Barter to Jab More Effectively

When you start your new business, you might not have the working capital to get things rolling. In fact, you might be living paycheck to paycheck in your 9 to 5, and that's part of why you feel trapped and why you can't ever escape "The Man." But there's always a way forward if you get a little creative.

One of the ways you *can* escape your job and build your business is with bartering. Let me explain.

Let's say you are an expert at growing herbs and vegetables. That's your thing. On your one-acre lot, you have the most incredible organic garden anywhere in your community. The thing to do is approach a local Mom and Pop restaurant that would use your produce in their cooking. Tell them you'd like to supply the herbs and spices for a cooking demonstration or cooking classes put on by them. In exchange, you'll get a little brand recognition for your organic herbs and vegetables within your small community. It's a start. It's small. Remember, baby steps here. We're not trying to become a multimillion-dollar corporation overnight—we're trying to build a small local brand with a real following.

Prior to the cooking class, you make a video of yourself talking about the herbs you're choosing for the class or picking the vegetables for the demonstration. Discuss the dishes the attendees will be making or tasting, and why you're choosing the produce you're picking—what these herbs bring to those dishes.

Create two or three 1-minute pieces and co-brand the restaurant in these pieces. If you don't have any budget for event promotion, you can post this as unpaid content to Facebook. Organic content is unpaid content—stuff that you publish to Snapchat or Facebook or Instagram that you don't put any marketing dollars behind. You just let it ride and people find it organically.

At the same time, you can have a conversation with the restaurant and say, "Hey restaurant, could you do me a favor? Are you going to promote this event on your Facebook page?" Yes? Great. "Could you hashtag my new business page, please? Or @ me?"

An @ means that if the restaurant posts on Facebook and your business has a Facebook page—which it should, by the way, what are you waiting for?—they'll simply use the @ symbol and begin typing the name of your Facebook page. Doing this will tag your page in their post and make it bold so people can find you. It's important because it gives love to your brand.

So now, even if the restaurant posts the event organically, if they have a following of 5,000 people or 20,000 people, every person who interacts with their brand that day is going to see *your* brand name and what's coming up. It gives these individuals an opportunity to click on your name and see your content as well. It's the circle of life again.

Let's say you've done all organic posts and the restaurant did all organic posts. You're both cross-promoting. You've got 100 followers; they've got 10,000. You've now got some brand-love from a powerful partner, and it didn't cost you anything except some time and some herbs.

Amp Up the Power of Barter with a Few Dollars

If the restaurant in our example here puts some marketing dollars behind your event, or if you have the ability to put some marketing dollars behind it, here is what you should do prior to the event: put a dollar a day behind each of those videos you created earlier and target a 15 or 20-mile radius around the event, depending on the geography of where you are. Target people who are interested in cooking or herbs or eating healthy using Custom Audiences on Facebook. It's a remarkable tool. Or, you just do Open Targeting and let Facebook decide for you.

Anyway, at the cooking event, offer a discount coupon for anyone attending the class to come pick their own herbs from your land, or get weekly deliveries of fresh herbs, or whatever it is you're doing with your business. You've just connected in a meaningful way with a dozen or more customers! And hopefully, had some fun at the same time.

Another Powerful Example of How to Barter for Growth

Let's say you've designed the most awesome clothing ever worn by any human being. You're an artist. Your dream has always been to create, or re-create, 80s album cover art on denim jackets and sell them. You've got jackets featuring Journey and Def Leppard and you want to start a Shopify store with these products but you don't have any photography skills or styling skills. You're afraid your photos are going to fall flat.

No problem—it's time to reach out to local photographers. Find a photographer in your neighborhood, and say, "Hey listen, I'm starting this new business. I need help with product photography, and I see from your Facebook profile that you're a fan of Pink Floyd. Would you be willing to help me with some product photography? In exchange, I will do my custom painted Pink Floyd *The Wall* jacket for you."

It costs you a little bit of material, it costs you your time, but at the end of the day, you have that anyway because this is what you do. So, you've just gotten product photography in exchange for a jacket. That's how this should and could go down.

I barter all of the time. When you don't have the capital, it's a great way to get ahead. When you do have the capital, it's a great way to conserve cash and get value for value from a business that you respect.

M&M Jabs

M&Ms are my favorite jab. Several years ago, M&Ms was looking for a new creative campaign for their My M&Ms, the custom M&Ms they produce as wedding favors or party favors. Together with my brilliant creative partner Sean Hughes, we created a concept that became an ad for them, they bought the ad rights and we produced the ad for them. That interaction became the basis of my most favorite and ongoing jabs to date.

When I have an exceptional customer experience, a great review from someone, an instance where a customer goes out of their way to thank us for what we do or I have a great experience with a vendor or a business that does something nice for us, I find their address. Maybe I know who the CEO is, or the person I dealt with, or the customer, and I order custom M&Ms that have little personalized messages for them and our branding on it. So, one group of candies might have the Ad Zombies head logo, and the rest have custom messages. People love it because it gives them an opportunity to see what I took away from, or remembered, about my unique relationship or interaction with them.

I will tell you, that jab goes so far because it's so personal and unique. I don't cheap out and just send them a bunch of M&Ms. I customize them for the interaction we had. It's a personal, thoughtful gift that brands the company. I can jab without an ask and still enjoy creating some value for my brand.

Jabbing Today and Beyond

You've found a couple of Facebook Groups that you're a part of. Let's say you're in a Facebook Group full of construction people, builders and other professionals in this industry. You are trying to leave your big corporate accounting firm. You want to start your own firm. A lot of questions are showing up in these Groups about the tax law changes and how it affects their companies. There's a lot of information being thrown around, but none of the individuals in this Group are tax professionals. You, on the other hand, are a tax savant. You understand the ramifications of the new tax law on their businesses, whether they're an LLC, an S Corp, a 501c3, whatever their status is.

Rather than saying, "Hey, Joe Builder, I'm starting my own business and I can help you," just give your advice in the group. "Hey everyone, I'm a tax professional. This is what I do for a living. Let me explain why you don't want to do this." Or, "Hey, in my 15 years as a tax professional, I can tell you that the changes will affect your business in ways that you haven't even thought of. In regards to your specific question, here are some things to consider." Now, you've come in and stated very clearly that you are a tax professional, but you're not pimping for business. What you're doing is adding value and helping these people.

If you don't think that this approach is going to make you rise to the top like the cream, you're wrong. It will. Everyone in that Group is going to have their attention on you. Next time someone jumps in with a question about accounting in their business or their tax liability, chances are very high that over a hundred people in that Group are going to say, "Talk to Jane Accountant. She's amazing, she knows everything." Guess what? You've started building your brand credibility.

How do you put that out there as content? Well, easy. "Hello, this is Jane Accountant. I was in a Facebook Group the other day, and a great question came up about the new tax law. It made me think that other businesses probably have the same question. So, here's my answer." Create that quick video. It's really easy to make that content because you're not producing it out of thin air. You're merely documenting what's already going on as you grow the business.

Get in those Groups. Jab and jab and jab and your brand will start to grow.

The Future of Jabbing

As more and more businesses realize the value of giving, rather than having this scarcity mentality, I think you will see more and more jabbing in the future. The reality is, the marketing profession is changing. The scarcity mentality that has existed since the beginning of marketing is starting to slowly erode. The big companies that are in control of messaging are starting to lose their power to smaller agencies that ad a lot more value. Many companies are realizing that they can do this shit directly to their customers.

The future of jabbing is very strong. If you always go into it with the intent of bringing more to the table than you're looking to walk away with, you're going to win. Big time. Giving is very powerful. I've often found that when I give of myself, I'm rewarded in ways I'd never even thought of. I jab for one company and get an introduction to a bigger company. I surprise and delight a customer with custom M&Ms, and they introduce us to an agency client who ends up spending thousands of dollars a month with us. It has a very powerful pay-it-forward feel to it. If you go into it with a pure heart, if you go into it with no expectations other than to bring value, you'll get way more than that in return.

Side note: Jabs are NOT "Free consultations" or "Free trials." A jab is a selfless act without expectation of reciprocation. Jabs are helping an old woman cross the street, returning someone's wallet, et cetera. They don't benefit you at all.

Entertaining Jabs

Not all jabs have a direct net positive effect on the recipient. In fact, sometimes it's a good idea to deploy a jab just for the sheer entertainment value of it. For example, many of the ads that we run for

Ad Zombies don't have an ask attached to them. Instead, our goal is to simply entertain the people who stumble upon our ad. Okay, they don't actually "stumble upon" our ad content; those ads are deliberately served to them. However, we are not going to bore them to death with messages that have asks attached to them. We are trying to build high-level awareness by providing things that make people laugh and things that make people feel good.

When our ads appear in a customer's newsfeed, or a potential customer's newsfeed, many times they don't even realize they are looking at an ad. What we are doing is creating an indelible mark in their brain, so we become the go-to for ad copywriting, or for any copywriting.

Think about this for a moment. Close your eyes and imagine you are in need of a few products. Let's say you have hemorrhoids. What would you go to the store and buy? Most people, by default, would buy Preparation-H, because it's the only brand they identify with the condition. If you had a cut on your finger and you wanted to put something on it to protect it, what would you use? A Band-Aid. But the reality is, it's a bandage. Band-Aid is the brand, but it's been so marked in your brain, it's hard to distinguish it from the product category. The final one: if you had a cold and needed to blow your nose, what would you use? A Kleenex. That's right, but it's not a Kleenex, it's a tissue.

Brand awareness creates that indelible mark in the brain that puts you first in the consumer's mind. Sales don't come through marketing, they come through brand awareness. It's very powerful to entertain and engage your audience at all times.

Give at Scale

As you build your dream business, remember to always give back. Give, give, give. Jab till it hurts. Do good things for people because it's the right thing to do, not because you're looking for brownie points or accolades.

For example, one Christmas Eve, my wife decided that she was done cooking Christmas Eve dinners and that we should go out to eat. So, we made reservations and took the family to Buca di Beppo for Christmas Eve dinner. We made a decision to do something very different that night. We decided to scope out the restaurant and find a family like ours—a family that had children or was large—and surprise and delight them. The way we did that was we schemed with our server to make sure that the bill for their table came to us. We then paid that bill. Instead of delivering a bill to their table, a Christmas card was delivered to that table with a handwritten note from my wife.

Now, every year the note is a little bit different, but it talks about how our family has been blessed and we just wanted to bless theirs with this simple gesture, and wish them a Merry Christmas and a Happy New Year. And that's it.

I have to tell you, this tradition has changed the way my children think. It has changed the way people in the restaurant behave when we come in. It has changed peoples' Christmas Eve, and I know we've touched so many lives over the years. It is so much fun to watch it unfold. In fact, when our favorite waiter left we were so disappointed that we were considering not doing it anymore. But we persevered, and every year we make that reservation.

We have the ability to give and do like this because of my business. It isn't lost on me that my business affords me the opportunity to do good for others.

You don't have to give monetarily, either. Prior to making this giving decision, my wife and I have done other things to give back to the community. We decided several years ago to become foster parents, and we wound up fostering 19 children and adopting three of them.

You can give back in so many ways. But just make sure you're always giving. If you give without any expectations of receiving, you will receive in an abundance. It's just the way the world works. I don't know if you believe in God or karma, or magnetism or whatever it is that causes this, but it just is true. When you give with no expectations, you receive in ways you never, ever dreamed of. So, don't ever stop giving, especially as your business grows. Because you will have the opportunity to give and give, and give.

Key Points from Chapter 6

- There's no such thing as too much jabbing.

- To create a memorable jab, connect with your audience's emotions.

- Leverage the power of barter to jab more effectively.

- Partner with other businesses on events and cross-promotion to increase the organic reach of your brand.

- Make your jabs personal and creative to impress your valuable customers.

- The future of marketing is jabbing.

Chapter 7: Mistakes

As you grow your business, you'll make mistakes. Forgive yourself. Then, read and re-read this chapter to avoid making more!

First of all, there's nothing more disingenuous to me than a business that approaches you with a jab that really isn't a jab. It's not a give; it's an ask. As you start your business, please be conscious of your jabbing. In the back of your mind, you must know that there is *nothing* coming your way from your give—and be okay with that.

Don't Disguise a Right Hook as a Jab

Too many people give with the expectation of receiving, but if you give with the expectation of just giving, you're going to be way happier. Sometimes you're going to give and get nothing, and sometimes you're going to give and get something amazing in return that you weren't even expecting.

When you offer a jab, don't have it be a right hook veiled in a jab. Have it be a true jab.

Often, companies reach out to me with their so-called jabs and they really are right hooks. I'll give you an example. Recently, there was an online conversation about credit card transaction processing and who uses what service, and I had commented that we processed X dollars a month through this one platform. Someone said, "I wouldn't use that platform, because a lot of times they have issues and they freeze money. I have a great card processor that I use for my online stuff. If you want me to connect you to them, let me know." Interested, I said, "Sure, send me some information." Well, they did. They sent me an affiliate link. Meaning, it's not that it's a great card processor. It means they get a kick-back. They get money or credit for getting another customer in their system. That's not a jab. That's a right hook.

When you are jabbing, make sure they are free jabs, and not attached to a right hook. Or it'll punch you right back in the face.

The Wrong Metrics

One of the things businesses do when they first start out is they begin buying ad space on Facebook or Instagram, YouTube, or whatever platform they choose. I beg of you: please think of your strategy in two ways. First, the cost of your day to day campaigns, your ads. Keep it affordable so you can continue it for a long time. Second, don't get hung up on vanity metrics like impressions or likes or any of those numbers, because you're in this for the long-term play. Likes and impressions don't matter. What matters is that you're getting in front of customers and building your brand.

If you're focused on the number of times people see your ad, you're focused on the wrong thing. What you want to do is create memorable impressions, and touch consumers many, many, many times. The more the consumer gets touched by your brand, the more they remember it—the more familiar you become. The closer you get to being the Preparation-H, the Band-Aid, the Kleenex of your category.

When you just focus on the numbers, you're going to lose out because you have to look big picture and look at the brand overall. Take the combination of creative and branding and marketing and put it all together with a long-term strategy instead of a short, narrow strategy.

If you say "I'm going to dedicate $5 a week to this," that won't get you anywhere. But if you say, "I'm going to put $1 per day behind this video and $5 behind that video and $10 to this one," the long-term strategy will play out. I'm not saying these are the actual budget numbers you should run. Please don't take that as gospel. It depends on your scale, it depends on what you do, it depends on your budget and on the depth and growth of your business. But, long-term strategy is what you should be thinking about and looking for.

Don't get hung up on the numbers. Get hung up on making an impression that sticks.

Can't Buy Me Love

When you first start your business, you might be tempted to "invest" money in building up some of those vanity metrics online. Look, we've all done it, and it's the wrong thing to do. I did it, and it was a terrible mistake. Why? Because they're not real. They're not real fans, there's no engagement from them. Vanity metrics may boost your numbers, but it's really doing nothing to boost your brand.

If you have 20,000 followers and you're a Matchbox collector who started a week ago, those numbers don't jive. It's okay to have 100 followers or 200 followers, because the ones that follow you and are genuinely connected to you are the people who are going to engage with your content and bring actual value to your business. They are the individuals who will help you grow.

Buying subscribers, buying shares whatever it is to build those vanity metrics is the wrong approach. You're going to be tempted to do it. Lots of you might even do it because it just looks so good. But it's all in your head and totally unnecessary. Save your money. Stop buying likes. It's doing nothing for your brand; it's doing everything for those companies who sell vanity metrics.

The Give is Better Than the Ask

I remember watching people in the restaurant industry, years ago, guard their secret recipes and special sauces. I thought, "God, that is so stupid. Why are you guarding this? People are never going to be able to make it to the same level and quality you do in the restaurant. You should just give it away!"

One day, I walked into a restaurant in Scottsdale, Arizona called Citizens' Public House. On the menu is this amazing chopped salad. In fact, the chopped salad is so famous it has its own Facebook page. Sure enough, when you walk into the restaurant and order the salad, you can also get a copy of the recipe. If you go online, to the Facebook page, you can get the recipe right there. Is the recipe ever going to taste the way it does when you order it at

Citizens' Public House? Hell no! Are they afraid of that? Absolutely not.

Just because you're giving something away doesn't mean you're hurting your business. I find the more I give, the more value I bring, the more I help people write their ads or fix their ads, the more people order ads from us. They love our service.

Giving is not going to hurt you. In the long run, giving is going to build your business.

I didn't always have a generous mindset. Once upon a time, I was probably the stingiest person when it came to giving and being selfless. Only over time have I learned the importance of it. I truly give credit to watching and learning from Gary Vaynerchuk. The man gives selflessly, and as he gives, I've watched his business explode. I'm just modeling what I've learned from the best. If you want to see your business grow, do the same. It will pay out in spades.

It Takes Balls to Get It Right—Bocce Balls

I met Kent Heyl, owner of Bocce Courts America. A client, Tom, who has become a friend over the years introduced me to him. Kent has an interesting business. Bocce courts, in case you didn't know, are making a comeback as a backyard entertainment, and people are getting Bocce courts installed in their yards in place of putting greens or swimming pools. Kent's company, Bocce Courts America, is a leader in Bocce courts for backyard entertainment.

I had a sit down with Kent. The first thing I looked at was all of this printed stuff he delivered for me to look at and review. I asked, "Who are you giving this stuff to?" He said, "Eh, no one. Because every time I give it to someone, they just throw it away." Well, *of course* they do! We're not living in the printed age. We're living in the digital age. Just ask the newspapers that have gone out of business. Only the smart ones like *The New York Times* figured out how to jump on the digital subscription model and grow.

I visited the website, boccecourtsamerica.com, and what's the first thing I see? Confusion. Because when a customer comes to your website, if your website doesn't clearly articulate what it is your business can do for them, what it is you sell, what service you offer, they're gone. If they're wasting calories and brain cells trying to figure out what it is you do, your messaging sucks. In this case, Kent's messaging was off target.

The headline when you arrived at the website was, "Do You Bocce?" It's a question. Well, fine, ask the question. But you're making a bold assumption that people know what Bocce is. And, I've got news for you, anyone who is not from the old world or is under 30 probably has *no freaking idea* what it is. None. So, the messaging has to be fixed. It's not, "Do You Bocce?" it's explaining Bocce in a quick and simple way.

Of course, there's no one sentence that can easily explain Bocce. So, it's about the lifestyle, about the entertainment, about the atmosphere that is created in your backyard when you have a Bocce court. Show *that* on the website. Put up a video, no sound is needed. In that video, you're going to show a Bocce court, and people having fun, and drinking wine and experiencing the outdoor lifestyle that this activity brings to the backyard. That's what this is about—a lifestyle. It's not about selling a dirt court with balls.

Figure Out if Your Business is B2B or B2C

The other fail on the Bocce website was the mixed messaging. When you're targeting a consumer audience, that is called B2C; you're the business, they're the consumer. When you're targeting a business audience, it's called B2B. They are two *totally different* audiences. You do not speak to them the same way. Kent's website is really confusing because it talks to both audiences equally. That's a disaster because consumers coming to the website looking for a Bocce court in their backyards are just not the same as businesses like hotels, homeowners' associations and high-end retirement communities.

When you are talking to these two audiences, there are two very different voices you should be crafting. If you're looking to grow your consumer first brand, your website needs to be geared toward them. Then the question arises: how do I talk to the businesses? Businesses will spend time, when they come to a website, to scroll to the navigation that is meant for them. Consumers will not. So, a couple of ways you can handle this is to create landing pages for your consumer audience and your business audience that come off of your ads. But the primary focus of your website should be consumer-facing. Then you have links, or navigation, for the businesses and what they might need, and all the options available to business customers.

If you're going to focus on consumers, you need to dial in that messaging so it's talking to that consumer audience. Yet the messaging is all over the place, right now, on boccecourtsamerica.com. As of the publication of this book, the website is a mess.

Kent wanted to know how a guy who started a business at 71—and he's now 78—can grow this business in two areas: the B2B side, selling the aggregate and the components; and the B2C side, selling more installations in people's backyards. Those audiences cannot cross over in marketing. They just can't. It's like having a conversation with your bro and having a conversation with your wife. You have to have two different voices when you speak to them. Consumers have one language, businesses have another language.

We had to create a plan for both business marketing and consumer marketing. You can target, by the way, businesses on both Facebook and LinkedIn. Consumers don't care about LinkedIn. For consumers, you'd want to use Facebook and Instagram. There's no other platform that's old enough to have the demographic who'd purchase these courts.

So, Kent's problem starts with his website, with the question "Do You Bocce?" But the real question is, *do you know what the hell Bocce is?*

Key Points from Chapter 7

- Don't disguise your right hooks as jabs.

- Don't buy followers or worry about vanity metrics.

- Figure out the targeting of your website content—are you a B2B or a B2C brand?

- Have a generous mindset.

Chapter 8: The Unintentional Pilot

I started this book with a question: Have you ever flown an airplane? About that question...

For many years, I joked that if I wrote a book, it would be called *The Unintentional Pilot,* the story about how I overcame my fear of flying. Entrepreneurship often comes with a nice big side of fear, regardless of when in life you start your business, so it's worthwhile to address it here. What are you afraid of? What are you doing to overcome it?

Before I dealt with my fear, flying was a big problem for me. For many years of my life, getting on an airplane was the single most horrifying thing I could do. I would have panic attacks, arrhythmias because I was so freaked out. I would have to take Valium, Vicodin, or something to be able to actually board. My hands would sweat. I would sit in silence on the airplane, I was just a terrified passenger. My heart was racing the entire time; I wouldn't eat or drink, let alone move out of my seat. It was debilitating.

Back when I was a creative director in the broadcast world, I was working with a great talk show host Preston Westmoreland. He came in one day and said, "Spanky, I gotta take you up in the plane, go up for a flight, to get over this fear you have. Because once you get up there, it's great." He and his wife Nancy spent all of their free time flying. They would do fly-in camping where they would fly to these fields in the middle of nowhere, and the lifestyle seemed like so much fun. But I would never do it, because the thought of getting in a plane *that small?* I already have problems getting into a commercial jet. No way.

Reluctantly, I agreed and we set up a date.

I felt if I could just go up in the plane once, maybe that would get me over my fear. I got in the plane, we took off, and I was holding on for dear life, I was white knuckling it. This thing had seats, it had power. It was a Piper Saratoga. The airplane was named the Christine 2, after the Stephen King book. So, great, I'm now in a possessed airplane. There was room for six, it was comfortable, but I was green and sweaty immediately. All of the things that raced through my head in a commercial jet were now racing through my head, and here I am sitting

149

only six feet away from the propeller. I'm watching the controls move right in front of me.

As we were flying toward the Superstition Mountains, Preston said, "Spanky, take the controls."

I froze, but I eventually grabbed the controls. I was so nauseous and I could feel my heart beating in my throat. I could feel the sweat. As I'm talking about it, I can still feel it, I can still remember that pure terror. There was nothing worse.

I had the controls, and I started to porpoise the airplane. That's what a lot of rookie pilots do—they correct a little too much, nose up, they correct a little too much, nose down. If you're looking at from the side, it resembles a porpoise swimming.

I was green and struck with fear, exhausted from the mental fatigue. I handed Preston the controls and we got back down on the ground at Williams Gateway airport, and he looked at me and said, "To get over this fear of flying, Spanky, you need to get with an instructor and go for a couple of lessons and get over that fear."

I said, "I have no intention of flying an airplane! Why the hell would I see an instructor?"

"It's not about flying," he said. "It's about getting over that fear of crashing or of dying, or whatever. You gotta go."

I discounted him, but a couple of days passed, and I realized my life was so limited by that fear of flying. There were so many places I wanted to go, and I had flown everywhere, but it took a lot to get me on a plane, and the night before I could never sleep.

So, I took his advice and ran with it. I found a flight school at Chandler Municipal Airport, and I made a phone call. This very nice gentleman, Butch Casdorph, answered the phone. He was retired from the Air Force and had just opened his flight school. I explained the situation and he said, "Okay, no problem."

We scheduled the appointment, I went to the airport, and we get into this Cessna 172, which is a really small plane compared to Preston's. I still remember the tail number: N734GY. We were ready to take off and he radioed the tower. We started rolling down the runway and off we went. We were up in the air and flew toward a practice area a few miles from the airport where there was no traffic.

As we flew, we chatted. I was in the left seat, the pilot seat.

He found out I was a creative marketing guy and said, "You know, I just opened my flight school and I could use some help with marketing." He proposed a nice way we could both help each other. "I'll help you get over your fear of flying, you help me with my marketing." It turned into a really cool relationship because I was just paying for fuel. Engine time and instruction were on him. It was really nice that I fell into that. Everything happens for a reason.

He asked me what my biggest fear was regarding the airplane. I told him it was crashing, that the engine would die and so would I. So, he pulled the power to the throttle back. The propeller was just wind-milling. There was no thrust.

The plane started to descend, and I'm screaming like you would hear a little girl scream when she sees a scary movie. That's me, as an adult, screaming at the top of my lungs.

The plane started to tilt nose down at a very gentle slope. We were in a controlled fall. Butch said, "Where could we put this thing down? Is there anything down there that looks like you could land the plane on it, should you need to in an emergency?" I looked down and saw a dirt strip.

"A runway is just a dirt road with lights," he said. "Let me show you what this looks like."

Pointing to a dial near the throttle he said "There's this thing in a plane called a trim wheel." He made a simple adjustment to the trim, dialed it in until our airspeed was 73 knots, and said, "I want you to take your hands off the controls for a second. Are we falling out of control?" We weren't. We were just gliding, slowly making our way down to the ground.

All of a sudden, he was touching down on this farm field, he gave it fuel. Then he lifted the flaps and we took off again. You have to understand that, physically, I was nauseous again, but I survived that moment in time. That ended my fear of, *If the engine fails, we're going to crash.*

Butch asked, "Did you have fun?"

"Not a bit," I answered.

We did a couple of these different maneuvers where I would tell him what I was afraid of, and he would do them—including a spinning descent. That ended my fear of crashing that way. When I got out of the plane, I literally kissed the ground like the Pope.

I started enjoying it and, with Butch's help, I continued to fly. I wanted to get on a commercial airplane and not have a single ounce of terror overcome me. One day, in early September, we were doing some landings and takeoffs, and he said, "Next landing, take it in." In other words, the instructor was telling me to solo: "You've got this."

153

We landed and I took the plane to an area of the airport called the "run-up" area. Butch grabbed my log book, signed something in it and said, "Now give me five takeoffs and landings, and I'll watch you from here. You don't need me, you've got this." The terror came back because now it was just me. He was telling me to take the airplane back up in the air and do this takeoff and landing sequence five times...by myself.

It was hard as shit, but I did my takeoffs and landings. When I landed the plane and met Butch on the tarmac, he was standing there with a pair of scissors. It's common practice in aviation for your instructor to clip the lower back portion of your shirt off as a sign of their newfound confidence in your piloting abilities. Butch cut the back of my shirt off. I soloed that day and it felt so amazing.

I had taken something I was so terrified of and turned it into a win.

Then I flew what's called a cross-country, at Butch's urging. It was going to take me to Yuma, to Blythe, California to refuel and eat a crappy lunch, then back to Chandler. The day came and I did it. Air traffic control communicated with me; there was traffic coming in and they vectored me around it. Two minutes later, I saw a jet fly by me at lightning speed. I thought to myself, *Wow, I didn't panic!*

Butch encouraged me to take the test and the check ride. So, I did it, and I became a pilot.

I never intended to become a pilot. I think sometimes people let their minds have so much control over what they do with their lives. My kids and I would fly to Sedona, I took some buddies for a guys' weekend in Vegas. I took my family to Bisbee, Prescott, I would fly wherever I wanted to for breakfast with the kids. Fear turned to fun.

I got over my fear by pushing myself out of my comfort zone. You *can* overcome what you're afraid of.

This is what it's like when you step out on that edge, that edge of *What the hell am I doing?* It's facing that same old fear that's been holding you back. It's irrational, it's scary. But if you push yourself, you just might find that you're piloting your own ship.

Let's Talk about So-Called "Security"

Many people are terrified to walk away from their corporate jobs. One of the things they think is, "Well, I've got job security, I've been here a long time, and I've got health care and 401k..." But the reality is, no job is safe. None. Zero. I have had friends who work for companies, and all they talk about is what they do, how critical they are, and yet they're not safe. I had one friend who was recently let go from a tech company he'd been with for 20 years. This was a guy who helped the company save millions and millions of dollars in their accounting, year after year, and yet was beached. You're going to give up your health care immediately when that happens unless you want to pay their COBRA fees.

None of those are reasons to stay stuck in a job you hate. Health care is a necessity for all of us. Everybody needs medical care and health insurance to protect themselves should they fall ill. But the truth is, we have insurance options. Are they all great? No. In the U.S. we have a marketplace, you can go buy insurance if you need it. We have the ability to go to any health care provider and be seen. If we pay cash, great. I'm not advocating *not* having insurance, but don't let something as simple as health insurance drive your decision making and keep you stuck in a place that you hate. Other countries have their insurance options, you're not married to your employer. Because, at the end of the day, working at a job that you don't like robs you of valuable years of doing your own thing, of *being you*, of finding happiness.

You can find health insurance and you can have your retirement plan roll into your own IRA or BizK. I've done it. All my 401k money from my corporate days is in my BizK. And, by the way, if you start your business practically and not fancy, you won't spend your retirement money building your business. You shouldn't do it. If you do that, I'm going to find you and beat the crap out of you because, in this day and age, it doesn't take much to start a business. A smartphone, a Squarespace website and a few Facebook Groups are all you need to launch. You don't have to dig into your savings to do this.

Shit, you don't even need business cards. If you want business cards, create the design on Canva and download it to your phone. When someone asks you for your card, just send it to them digitally and share your contact information.

What if you didn't take the chance? Will you be sitting there at the end of your life regretting that you didn't believe enough in yourself? Regret is a horrible thing. I can't imagine, at the end of my life, regretting that I didn't try something, didn't do something. That I didn't step off the ledge and take that chance, not knowing what was in front of me. Just because you're approaching retirement age doesn't mean you need to approach everything like you're frail. Approach it with gusto! Supercharge your retirement. Bring in more money than you've ever brought in before, in your life. The only regret you'll have is that you didn't do it sooner.

Overcoming Business Fears

You already read about how I overcame my fear of flying. The same rule applies to business. You put your head down and you hit the GO button.

But the fear that I have most is failing my family. What does that look like? It looks like not being able to feed my children, or not being able to provide for them a life that is better than what I had. Failing is letting them down and has nothing to do with me and has nothing to do with the business.

I have this deeply rooted need to be the Tarzan of my family. I am the hunter, I am the gatherer. It is my job to do that for them. After my first two children were born, my wife and I became foster parents. We went on to foster 19 children. Our three youngest were adopted by us. I have this deeply personal need to provide for all of my kids and to make sure that their needs are met. Failing, to me, is failing *them*. That's my motivator every day, my driving factor. My family will *never* starve. My family will never want for the things they need to survive and live. For me, that's the only thing I think about and worry about. It helps that I live practically. We don't have debt; we have a house. We don't live above our means.

Most people have fear over things they have no control over, or things they make up in their heads before they even take a chance on it. They'll talk themselves out of even starting a business because they think *"What if it fails?* I've always wanted to do my photography business, but what if it fails?"

And? What if it fails? Then what?

Would you rather have the *fear* of failure, or would you rather have a failure? I'd rather have a failure—because that means I'm 0 for one and not 0 for 0. At least I tried. I did something. I stepped out of the comfort zone, I took a chance. I'll gladly fail six times as long as I get up seven times.

That's how you overcome those fears. It's just like flying. Get into the cockpit and *start to control it.* The outcome is based solely on you and the decisions you make. It's easy. Fear shouldn't control you. It should be the motivator. It should be what makes you tick.

Key Points from Chapter 8

- Be honest with yourself about your fears, and be willing to confront them head-on.

- There's no such thing as "job security."

- There are ways to secure health insurance and put together a workable retirement plan without a regular salaried job. Don't let your attachment to your benefits stop you from starting a business.

- Don't let fear control you.

- There's no reason to spend a lot of money when you start your business. Be practical.

Chapter 9: A Successful Entrepreneur

There's one quality that I believe determines whether someone will be successful, or whether they'll fail in whatever endeavor it is they're pursuing. It's *tenacity*. I have a relentless tenacity that is so visible to everyone. My wife talks about it, my friends talk about it.

Failure doesn't exist for me, because it's not an option for me. Besides tenacity, the other quality many entrepreneurs share, in my opinion, is the desire to always do more, to one-up themselves. See, for me, everything is a game. Let me explain. Sales days begin for us at 12:00 AM—every day, the calendar resets at midnight. So, let's say we start rolling in sales early in the day and we hit $1,000 in new business sales by 3 AM. For me, it's not a financial thing. It's not about the $1,000, the question is can we do $2,000 by 6 AM? $10,000 by the end of the day? It's a game to me. It's always wanting to one-up what we just accomplished.

Seeing business as a game and seeing it as fun is a nice way to grow. It's not about dollars and cents, it's about doing better than before and achieving something that we have not yet achieved. I don't necessarily size people up, what I do is listen to them, and what they're doing. Just based on the way they talk, or the way they position what it is that they're doing, it's pretty easy to determine if they're on the right path or not. They may succeed by accident, or they might fail because of poor planning. But the reality is most entrepreneurs are dreamers, living way, way in the future. They don't spend a lot of time in the past. They don't spend a lot of time reminiscing or putting out fires in the day-to-day. They envision tomorrow and dream about what will be.

My First Business

Entrepreneur wasn't a word when I was a kid, but I knew I was different. I always knew that I was different—not in a good way, at times. I was a terrible student, *terrible*. Part of it was that I was bored. School didn't challenge me, and most of the crap I was taught was useless, like teats on a bull to me, and I just thought school was a complete waste of my time. To this day, I still believe that our school system is busted beyond belief, and is a waste of most of our kids' time, and doesn't teach them anything.

Anyway, it was 1979. I was 12 years old, and there was a gas shortage in the United States because of something going on with OPEC. There was rationing of gas. People could only get gas on odd numbered days, or even numbered days depending on your license plate number. The lines would extend for miles because there was this shortage.

There I was in Queens, New York, growing up right off of Union Turnpike and 166th Street—shout out to the people of Queens—and, the first or second day, I saw the lines forming, and asked my mom what they were. My mom explained, and so I decided to take my bike down to Kissena Boulevard, to Buddy's Bike Shop. I had gone there a lot because I was into bikes, and BMX was starting to become a thing. All I wanted to do was ride. Anyway, I said, "Buddy, I need your help. Could you put all of the baskets you could possibly configure onto my bike?" I came back the next day, and he had done it. I didn't have the money to pay for this, but I told him I would work it off. He was super cool about it. I don't think my parents ever knew this part. This is the first time I shared this little detail.

Anyway, I got the baskets, and the next morning at 4:30 AM, I was working the gas line on my bike offering coffee, donuts and newspapers to the people in the line. I didn't charge them a service fee, they paid for what they ordered and I just worked for tips. I quickly figured out that I could get Dunkin' Donuts a little cheaper if I pre-ordered. I started to get into the rhythm of knowing how many donuts I would need each day. At 12 years old, I was making thousands of dollars a week. That was my first business venture. I was providing a service people needed—I had a solution that would make their day better. Money was a side effect, benefit of the service.

My Daily Habits

My habits are a little bit strange, but I think part of what works for me is my routine.

My new daily routine is getting up at 5 AM, having my coffee, and getting in the gym by 5:30. My quiet time to think is spent on the treadmill doing my cardio. Working with a personal trainer has helped me lose weight, get in better shape (for me), and has given me even more energy than I've ever had.

What I then do is shower, and ideas start to flow when I'm in the shower. When I get out, I jot them down immediately. When I have a shower thought, and I do call them shower thoughts, I will lose them the moment someone talks to me or my focus shifts. I know I will forget some really great ideas before I get the chance to write them down if I don't do it right away. Now that I have Amazon devices all over my home, it makes it easier. Alexa has changed my world because I could walk to any room in my home and say, "Alexa, take a note," and it will drop it in a To Do list for me automatically.

For me, mornings are the most productive for idea generation and organizing my day. I really need that quiet time. I find news to be very distracting, music to be very distracting. I just like silence and my coffee.

The Sweat of Regret

I was on summer vacation with my family in Southern California when, at 4 AM one morning, it hit me: I don't want to have regrets about would've, should've, and *could've*. At 51, I realized that if I make it to 80, that only gives me 29 more years on Earth to accomplish my goals. That is nothing! 29 more years to get to where I want to be, to make things happen, to make the world a better place for my kids, for my family, for my legacy.

If you are the same age I am, 51 or 50 or 45 or 60, and you're still wanting to achieve great things, or little things, or important things to you, please,

please don't wake up in the sweat of regret. It's scary as shit to step off the pier and not know if you can swim, but I'm telling you, you can figure this shit out. And the longer you stay doing the thing you don't like doing, the more you're going to wake up in the sweat of regret.

There is nothing worse than being at the end of your life and wishing you had done this or that or the other thing. I remember when my grandfather, Lou, was about a week away from taking his last breath, we were talking about the things he never got to do in his life, things he had always wanted to do. One of them was visit the Great Wall of China. He wanted to go to China and take this amazing trip—and never got to do it. I promised him that *I* would take that trip, that I would see the Great Wall of China. I had no desire, at the time, to see the Great Wall of China, but I said, "Grandpa, I will go. I will see this thing that you never got to see." He had deep regret because he put it off to accommodate others in his life. He put it off to make sure everyone else was provided for, that everyone else's needs were met.

I just want to remind you that there's nothing wrong with being selfish once in a while. Because what I'm really talking about here is not actually selfish at all—because the happier you are, the more productive you are, the better off your entire family will be.

I also remember when my father-in-law John was diagnosed with cancer. As the end of his life drew closer, a regret surfaced. One of the things that he had always regretted was not taking all of the kids, spouses and grandkids to Disney World. He wanted to do this amazing family trip. Not everybody wanted to do it, but had he pushed for it, it would've happened. I know that was a regret for him that he never got to do this thing with his grandkids, all of the grandkids together—because he didn't push for his dreams, for his goals, for his life's ambition. That was something that *he* wanted to do.

Too many people die with regrets. They die with unfinished business. Now's your opportunity to finish that business. Now's the opportunity for you to make that change, to live life on your terms. Don't wake up in the sweat of regret.

Better Than Sex

Sure, sex feels great. But the intense pleasure doesn't really last that long. You can't feel the climax all day, every day. So, what feels better than sex? How about helping someone achieve their goals? This idea isn't like some Miss America statement to win a competition, either. Helping others really does feel better than sex, and the pleasure is constant. This has been one of the biggest takeaways for me since I launched Ad Zombies: the ability I have to help others in their businesses is so personally fulfilling, it's not even funny.

When you start your business, your brand, whatever it is you do, if you're an expert in a certain area where others are not, you have the unique ability to help them, to give value in ways that other people just can't. The ability to help somebody achieve their goals, the ability to give someone something, to jab, and to help is so awesome, and it feels so damn good.

There is nothing better. There is no high that is better, there is no sex that is better than being able to help someone. So, as you start down your journey to take that leap, and to make big changes in your life, to do your thing, and to create your version of whatever it is you're going to do, remember as you go to help people along the way. Be helpful. Give of yourself freely. Continue to do so every single day, because it feels so great, and pays you back in so many ways that you don't even realize. Giving like this, helping someone achieve their goals, feels way better than sex.

Key Points from Chapter 9

- One quality that will serve you well as you start and grow your business? Tenacity. Don't quit.

- Get up early each day and devote time to simply thinking and jotting down ideas.

- Don't wake up in the sweat of regret later in life by failing to act now.

- Nothing feels better than helping people achieve their goals. As you grow, keep giving and helping.

Conclusion

I have now gone over the manuscript of this book five or six times. I've had my Apple computer read the manuscript to me at least a dozen times. I realize it might sound repetitive at times, but I cannot stress enough that in order to achieve, you have to take action. Many people will read this book, or listen to the audiobook and be motivated or inspired, yet they'll do nothing. I don't know if it's a human nature thing, or what, but Gary Vaynerchuk said this to me at dinner: "I can give away all of my best advice for free to people, and only a very small percentage, maybe one percent, will put it to use, will take action."

It's Not the End, It's the Beginning

I hope this book inspires you to be that one percent. Maybe I'll get lucky and hit two percent. But I hope it inspires you to realize that whatever you think you can do, or whatever you dream of doing, you can do. There are no more shackles on you. The man doesn't own you. It's time for you to lose the floaties, jump off the pier, and learn to swim. Because once you start swimming, you'll discover there's a massive ocean waiting for you.

Acknowledgements

You would not be reading this book were it not for the people who touched my life at the right moment.

Thank you to Gary Vaynerchuk for not only being a great entrepreneur but for inspiring me and millions of people around the world to do what's in their hearts. Your mentorship and advice have proven invaluable, and I appreciate everything you do and have done for me. Your level of give a shit is amazing. The time you take to answer my questions, to guide, to help...is remarkable.

To my operations ninja and friend Brandon Disney. You are my magic button maker, and the guy who makes things happen. Without you, my life would be full of manual processes and misery.

To Russ Hill, you exemplify leadership. Knowing you and learning from you has been an honor, and if, over the next forty years of my life, I could become half of who you are as a person, I will have achieved incredible growth.

To Cat Howell. Cat, your willingness to let me ask questions of your online community is what started this business. Ad Zombies would not have taken its first breath without your willingness and openness. I am forever grateful.

Sean Hughes, you were there from day one of Wedgie Media, and you were there the day Ad Zombies came to life. While I may have been the second best man at your wedding, you have always been my number one pick to be my number two guy. Thank you for everything you do.

To Casey Carroll, you are an amazing brand strategy partner, but your math skills are a total disappointment. ;)

Thank you also to the amazing staff at the Courtyard Phoenix Gateway Airport for allowing me to utilize the back of your awesome lobby as my private book-writing space.

To the members of my private group of elite entrepreneurs who hold me accountable and create an awesome group of friends, thank you:

Robin Alex
Lee Bradshaw
Larry Brooks
Casey Carroll (still mathematically challenged)

David Carroll (not related to Casey, he can add)
Baldeep Chawla
Jared Fabac
Joe Giglietti
Brenda Kelley
Josh Kelly
Philippe LeCoutre
Chris Patterson
Joe Rizzo
Nik Robbins
Damien Rufus
Adam Sand
David Tash
Tom Tran
Carson Young

Cover design for this book was done by my friend and colleague, Jeff Minnichbach, owner of No Limit Creatives, <u>NoLimitCreatives.com</u>. Thank you.

Cover photo by Chris Matsuno, @matsunophotography. Thank you.

Last but not least, thank you to the most important person in the making of this book, my incredible ghostwriter Laura Schaefer, <u>LauraSchaeferwriter.com</u>. You took the words right out of my mouth and brought them to life.

Made in the USA
San Bernardino, CA
31 October 2018